As you close this pivotal chapter of life, and embark on the next, We offer you this tale of resilience, courage, and commitment - In her story, may you find the inspiration to write your own.

W9-CTY-728

If You Save One Life

If You Save One Life

A Survivor's Memoir

THE
Upper
Story
PRESS

Published by:
Upper Story Press
1551 Reeves Street
Los Angeles, California 90035
Email: info@upperstorypress.com
Web: www.upperstorypress.com

ISBN 978-0-9793582-7-2

Library of Congress Control Number: 2007934487

Learn more at www.evabrown.org

Set in Palatino Linotype
Printed in the United States of America
Cover art by Chaim Singer-Frankes

For my family,
past and present

Acknowledgements

I HAVE WAITED MORE than six decades to tell my story. I could not have done so without help from many people. First and foremost, I thank my family—Nancy and Kimberly, Sandy and Steve—for their constant love and support. Paul Soroudi has provided the sort of compassionate friendship for which every person wishes.

I will always be grateful to the staff of the Museum of Tolerance, who gave me the opportunity and the platform to tell my story to thousands and thousands of strangers who became my friends. I am indebted to the audiences: students, teachers, tourists and so many others who have taken the time to listen to me and, often, to share part of themselves in return.

Tom Fields-Meyer, my co-author, is a tireless listener and talented writer who, over our many hours together, became a trusted friend. I am indebted to Paul White, teacher at West Valley Leadership Academy in Canoga Park, California for his friendship and for inspiring me and helping me find Tom. Marc Porter Zasada of Upper Story Press had the imagination and skills to bring my dream to reality. Thanks to the many people who read drafts and provided valuable insights and suggestions: Shawn Fields-Meyer, Lora and Jim Meyer, Daniel Gordis, Ron Arias, Mary Hanlon, and Andrea King.

I am grateful to El Camino College in Torrance, California where I am honored to have a foundation fund in my name to help provide materials for teaching about the Holocaust and tolerance issues.

I also want to give special thanks to Gerald Adler, talented professor of cinema, who has recorded much video of my presentations and created an everlasting legacy.

Finally, I am forever indebted to the two most important men in my life, my late father and late husband. I miss them both dearly and I feel that they are holding my hands, giving me the strength to continue to do what I do every day.

Contents

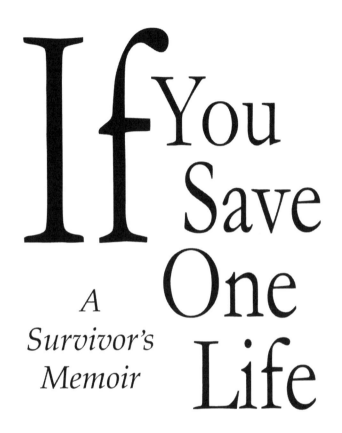

If You Save One Life

A Survivor's Memoir

Eva Brown

with Thomas Fields-Meyer

If I am not for myself, who will be for me?

And if I am only for myself, what am I?

—Hillel

Prologue

ONE MORE DAY AND I WOULD likely be dead. I was barely clinging to life. I was 17 years old and weighed no more than 65 pounds. After nearly a year as a prisoner of the Nazis, I had endured two weeks of a forced march that my captors surely hoped would finish me off for good—two weeks trudging through the rain, denied water or food; two weeks of subsisting on insects, wild mushrooms, and whatever else I could gather along the roadside. Typhus was destroying my body, sapping my strength and causing a burning fever and painful rashes. After months of deprivation and abuse, I could barely move.

And then, just after dawn broke on a brilliant May morning, I spotted a tank bearing an insignia I had not seen in all those months: an American flag.

As a column of tanks surrounded me—and the hundreds of other forsaken Jews with me on that long, brutal journey—soldiers emerged and simply stared at us, undoubtedly shocked to encounter in the wooded German countryside a parade of the walking dead.

They spoke English. I understood only one word they said.

"Freedom."

As the American soldiers passed canteens of water and tossed chocolate bars, German officers scurried away, trying to slip into the dense cover of the forest.

Amid all the chaos, one of the Americans stepped toward my group, speaking a familiar tongue.

"Kenst du redn Yiddish?" he said—Does anyone speak Yiddish?

I raised my hand.

He told me he was from the Bronx, New York. He assured me that medical care was on the way—that we would be taken care of. Then he looked at me, taking in my gaunt, shrunken body, and put a hand on my shoulder as I shook from exhaustion.

"Point a finger," he said, "at the one who made you look like a skeleton."

EVERY TUESDAY I TELL MY STORY—to high school kids, to church groups, to police cadets and educators. Riding a taxi the three miles from my Los Angeles home to the Simon Wiesenthal Center's Museum of Tolerance, I take an elevator to the second floor, walk down a corridor to a small auditorium, take my place behind a podium, and scan the audience. I stretch my frame to my full height—five feet— and begin, always with the same words:

My name is Eva Brown. I'm going to take you on a long journey, all the way back to Hungary, where I was born in 1927…

And for nearly an hour they listen—the teenagers, the retirees, the Christians and Hindus and, sometimes, Jews. I describe an idyllic childhood in the small town of Putnok, where my father was the rabbi, and how the Nazis destroyed that community; how I endured Auschwitz, labor camps, the death march; and how I somehow managed to survive a war that claimed the lives of all but 6 of my sixty-six relatives.

I have spoken to more than 1,000 audiences, and thousands have written letters to express how their lives have been changed by my words. I have told my story in churches and as words of inspiration at schools where most of the students have long criminal records and little hope. I have shared my tale as a college commencement speaker, though I never made it past sixth grade.

But for decades I could not tell my story. I was silent, holding tightly to the secrets of what I had seen, heard, and endured.

My husband, too, was mute on the topic—and for good reason. The Nazis had murdered most of Ernie's family. And he saw no value in dredging up the horrors he had experienced at Buchenwald and Mathausen.

Instead, we made a life in America, learned the language, raised two children and made a living. When my young daughters would ask about the tattoo on my left forearm, I told them it was my Social Security number. In time they would sense there was something deeper lurking, but I wasn't ready to share it.

But my silence did not keep the memories at bay. Even as I built my life, the past haunted me, never leaving my mind for a day. Not even for an hour. I was tormented.

On the worst days of the war I had willed myself to live with a promise I had made myself: that when all of this was over, I would tell the world. I would spread the story of what the Jewish people had endured, and how—despite it all—we survived. I believed that was God's mission for me.

That made the silence more painful.

Then came a dream.

One night in my forty-third year I awoke with a start. It was different from the nightmares that had always brought me back to the terrifying scenes of those dark years. This time, my mother came to me—my blessed mother Rozsi. She was young and pretty, with hands just like mine, and wearing a *sheitl*, the wig Orthodox women would wear.

"Leah," she said, using the Hebrew name that few had called me in decades. "Leah, did you get the schmaltz?"

Stirred from my sleep, I was brought back to 1943. With the Nazis threatening to occupy Hungary, the Jews of Putnok were preparing for the worst. Daily, the government would announce new edicts and food rations. Police routinely searched homes for violations, exacting frightening punishments. Still, our friends and neighbors hid cash in their attics and concealed silver beneath floorboards to be retrieved after the war.

My mother—ever practical and always a mother first—had another idea.

"We have little children." She told my father. "When winter comes, we won't need our silver. But we will have mouths to feed."

In a Jewish home in Hungary in the 1940s, cooking required schmaltz—fat from a goose or a chicken. Without that, how could Mother make the smorgasbord she put on our Sabbath table almost every Friday night and Saturday afternoon I could recall? In the kitchen, Mother scooped the golden, buttery schmaltz into a purple ceramic crock, sealed the top and wrapped it in a towel. As the sky darkened, my father and I stepped out behind the house. I stood guard while he shoveled a hole, then placed the crock in the ground, covering it with soil. It was our secret—a buried treasure. Or the closest thing we had.

I had not recalled that evening in years—until I was startled to consciousness in my Los Angeles home and woke up my husband.

"Oh my God," I told Ernie. "I forgot about the schmaltz!" Only days later, the two of us flew to Budapest, then took a train the 150 miles to Putnok. There, we found the place where my home once stood. It was now part of a pottery factory, but I was able to find the precise spot where my father dug the hole—now paved over with concrete—and explained to the manager why I had come. He threatened to call the police. He shouted at me. Menacing dogs began circling.

"Okay," my husband said. "You tried. You answered your mother's question. Here is your schmaltz."

In so many ways, my life has been a struggle to get back what was taken from me—my beautiful childhood, my close and loving family, an entire way of life. And just as I could not recover the crock of goose fat, I cannot retrieve the people I lost. I cannot recover the girlhood that was so cruelly interrupted.

I lost so much, but I held on to one gift: memory. I survived with a sacred purpose: to tell my story.

I tell it to keep alive the memory of my parents—who instilled in me the faith that helped me survive—and of the rest of my family. For I am the last one left. I share my story as a way of speaking for my 60 dear ones who perished and for the six million who have no voice.

This mission has given my life renewed meaning and purpose—and inspired others.

"I recall moments in my life when I was faced with obstacles that made me feel hopeless," a student wrote me in one of the more than 2,000 letters I have received from people who have heard my tale. "My experiences were nothing compared to yours and you still have the courage to move on."

Those who hear my story almost always react with surprise—and wonder—to a single moment in my life: that morning on the outskirts of Munich in the spring of 1945, when, near death, I faced the American soldier and he told me in Yiddish to point to the perpetrators.

Not a day passes when I don't think about the response I gave him. For it was rooted in everything that had come before. And what I said to him gave me the freedom to go on to lead a full and meaningful life. It has given me a measure of peace. That moment, when I was only 17 years old and I had already endured so much, was a turning point that reflected and manifested my beliefs and transformed everything I have done since.

"It left me in awe," one college student wrote me, "of your ability to see good in this world."

If my words have kept memory alive, I am grateful. If they inspire others, I am humbled. I can only pray that this volume does the same.

1

A Rabbi's Daughter

EVERY FAMILY HAS ITS TREASURES: the heirloom engagement ring; the sterling tea set; grandfather's antique pocket watch. When I was a girl, my family's two most cherished possessions were both books.

One was my father's *siddur*, the Hebrew prayer book he used to *daven*—to pray—every day. Worn from almost constant use (Jews pray three times a day, and as a rabbi, Father rarely missed the opportunity), it also contained a precious list. Inside the front leaf, Father had scrawled the Hebrew names of every living member of our extended family. On Shabbat afternoons, I would sit comfortably in Father's lap, reading and re-reading that list: my mother, father, their parents, my aunts, uncles, cousins. It seemed never to end. I was nine when my youngest brother, Viktor, was born. After the *bris,* I watched Father add his Hebrew name to the list in tidy Hebrew script: "Herschel. February 1937."

"There," Father said. "Now there are 67 people in our *mishpoche*" —our family.

Our other cherished book was a diary. Father had spent four years serving in the Austro-Hungarian army, defending the country's freedom in the First World War. He earned five medals for distinguished

18

service, and he was as proud and patriotic as any citizen. In the green leather-bound journal, he had chronicled his service, recording in his neat, looping handwriting his adventures on the Italian front, where he learned fluent Italian (and where being an Orthodox Jew was never an obstacle; an Army chaplain gathered Jewish soldiers to pray in a minyan each morning, helped acquire kosher food and made sure he got leave for the holidays). When I was young, we would gather around and listen to Father read entries from his diary, regaling us with tales of bravery and valor.

All my life I have loved books—their texture, their feel in my hands, the infinite worlds they contain. But if I could get back any two, it would be those: the family prayer book and the diary. For if they were precious then, on the eve of the Second World War, they would be all the more sacred now. They contained so much that was lost.

I was born August 24, 1927, the fourth of my parents' seven children. We were the fifth generation of my family born in Hungary. My parents and grandparents were all devout Jews and equally committed Hungarian citizens. No matter how religious they were, they considered themselves Hungarians first and Jews second.

My father, Solomon Rosenfeld—Shloyme to my mother and Reb Shloyme to everyone else—eagerly anticipated every national holiday, when he would march through the town square with local officials, followed by hoards of schoolchildren, to celebrate Hungary's freedom. He would don his full military regalia, complete with his medals (carefully polished by my mother), carrying the Hungarian flag and beaming with delight.

I was born in Hajdúböszörmény, a small town 150 miles east of Budapest. At the time, my parents were living with my mother's mother and her father, who ran a business selling feathers and leather. Grandfather—we called him Zayde Yitzhak—had an easy, natural way with children. He would tease us all with the same riddle: "Which weighs more," he would ask, "a pound of leather or a pound of feathers?" He fooled us every time.

My earliest memory is of a lovely Saturday afternoon I spent with

Zayde Yitzhak when I was three years old. Every Shabbat afternoon, he would walk the quarter mile to the synagogue for *mincha*, the brief afternoon prayer service. It was his custom to bring two small, braided loaves of bread, the *challahs*, for the small meal between the afternoon and evening services. I had watched from week to week as my older siblings enjoyed the privilege of accompanying him for the stroll. But one week, Zayde handed me the challahs. "Come with me, Leah," he said, using the Hebrew name everyone in my family called me. It felt like a great honor that my turn had finally come, and I walked with pride beside my Zayde, cradling the challahs.

The warmth and richness of Judaism had long attracted my father, too. After he completed the army, Father had gone to *gymnasium*—a junior college—and then went to yeshiva, where he became absorbed in the world of Jewish texts and studied to become a rabbi. I was three when he completed his yeshiva studies and started looking for a congregation. Three different shuls offered him positions, and when he couldn't decide which offer to accept, he consulted with his own rabbi. His advice sent my parents and their five children (two more came along later) to Putnok, a town of 3,000, where at the age of 37, Father became the rabbi for the area's 250 Jewish families.

Putnok was a peaceful farming community on a fertile plain in northeastern Hungary between the river Sajó and the Carparthian Mountains. The soil was rich, the air and water were clean and pure, and the climate was harsh in every season. We shoveled snow in the winter, slogged through mud after spring's torrential rains, sweated through blazing summers, and endured windy autumns. But it had the best of everything: bread, poultry, and beef. Farming was the town's largest industry by far, but most of the Jewish men ran businesses. They were shoemakers or tailors; some were educators.

The synagogue Father took over was a modest, cream-colored stone structure with high ceilings inside and a balcony where the women would sit. The carpeting was a beautiful wine color, the woodwork was gorgeous and well maintained, and the holy ark held perhaps 20 Torah scrolls. The *shul* shared a courtyard with a few smaller structures. The schoolhouse had three rooms for the public school I attended in the morning and, on the other side, one large classroom for our afternoon Hebrew classes. Nearby were a house for the cantor and another for the *melamed*, a tall, gentle man named Yankel Weisz, who oversaw our Jewish education. The Weiszes had eleven children. My siblings and I entertained ourselves by competing to see who could recite all eleven of their names in order. (I remember them to this day!)

Nearby was our home, a one-story beige stucco house with a red tile roof. The nine of us shared three bedrooms, so I always shared with one or two sisters, and my parents had a child or two in their own room. That was common—none of my friends had their own bedrooms—and it felt comfortable. Father spent much of his time in his small den, which was lined with Hebrew volumes—Torah commentaries, tractates of the Talmud, all kinds of mystical texts. In any extra space we had, Father would put a bookshelf.

My mother, Rozsi, presided over a compact, kosher kitchen: one set of dishes for meat, another for dairy meals. Like most Hungarian homes, ours also had a summer kitchen, a semi-open area for preparing food when warm weather made it uncomfortable indoors. We didn't have running water; we carried water for drinking and washing from a well behind the house. (The toilet was an outhouse in the back.) Mother did everything by hand—washing, cooking, cleaning—with the assistance of two household helpers, Molly and Terry, Hungarian peasants who practically raised us and became like members of the family. (Putnok's few wealthy Jewish families hired German nannies to care for their children. It was considered a status symbol and since the Yiddish spoken in most Jewish homes was similar to German, communication was easy.) Outside was a lush garden the neighbors all shared. Just outside our home we grew beautiful flowers and just beyond that were vegetables and fruit trees.

I spent most of my childhood in that safe, comfortable cocoon, where the highlight of the week was Shabbat dinner, when we would all gather to share Mother's seemingly endless array of specialties: chicken soup with matzah balls, farfel, fish, meat, goulash, all kinds of fresh vegetables—and my favorite, poppy-seed noodles.

Father always invited one or two of the young students who studied Talmud with him. He never wanted anyone to spend Shabbat alone, so we always had widows and widowers at the table. My grandparents on both sides visited Putnok frequently for one occasion or another—bar mitzvahs, holidays, summer vacation—so they would eat with us too.

At the Shabbat table, my parents' rule was that only Yiddish was spoken. That was the law and we abided by it. (The rest of the week my parents spoke Yiddish to each other, but we children primarily spoke Hungarian; yet, though we all had Hungarian names, we mostly used our Hebrew names.) Zayde used to smile and ask the children: *"Kanst du redn Yiddish?"*—Can you speak Yiddish? I would say, "Yes." And he would say *"Vos kenst du zogn?"* —What can you say?

It was a home full of warmth and security. Music was a big part of our lives. Father liked to play the violin and my oldest brother, Andor, had a beautiful baritone. (I never had much of a voice, but I loved to listen and even had a taste for opera.) We would sit together and sing and dance with such joy that sometimes Mother would shut the window and beg us to keep quiet.

"If anyone from the synagogue board passes by and sees us singing and dancing, your father will never get a raise," she would say. "They'll say, 'The rabbi's family is doing so well, he doesn't need it.'" She was only partly joking. But the raises always came.

I can still picture the faces around the Shabbat table: Father at the end, a strong, sturdy man with a full, black beard and a large black yarmulke, gorgeous brown eyes and dark complexion. Mother was just over five feet tall, with brown eyes and a warm, lovely smile. During the week it seemed she always had an apron on, but on Shabbat she would wear a dress and *sheitl,* a wig.

My oldest brother, Andor (his Hebrew name was Yosef), was six years older than I, and he had such a beautiful singing voice that as a teenager he became a professional cantor, moving to Budapest when he was 17 to take a full-time job with a congregation. Even as a child, Andor was self-assured and very social.

Irene, two years younger, was almost his opposite. Short, with beautiful green eyes, she was good natured and generous, but also withdrawn and shy. She was like a mother to the rest of us children, pitching in with the cooking and sewing dresses. Irene was in charge of birthday parties. (We always made homemade ice cream, since Putnok's ice cream parlor wasn't kosher.)

Aranka, two years Irene's junior, didn't like doing domestic work (Mother had to remind her to clean up after herself), but she was skilled with her hands. She was the social one, always surrounded by a circle of friends.

My brother Sandor was a beautiful child with the most gorgeous brown eyes. "His eyes are like velvet," Mother used to say. Sandor was everybody's sweetheart—loveable and likeable and smiling all the time. Sandor was two years younger than I was and he was always well behaved in school and at home.

Valerie was four years younger than I. She was cute and pretty. The two of us were very close, spending long hours playing dollhouse. I would sew clothes for her little dolls. I loved to comb her straight, brown hair and tie bows in it.

Viktor—we called him Hershel—was the baby of the family. I was nine when he was born and I was an almost maternal presence for him. The summer after he was born, Mother went to visit her parents for two weeks and left the baby at home, knowing that I would take responsibility. We had a babysitter, but my job was to take care of his emotional needs. (As a thank-you gift, Mother brought me the most wonderful polka-dot dress and headbands in every color.) Viktor had beautiful blond locks; in Orthodox families the tradition was not to cut the boys' hair for the first three years, so I used to spend hours combing it, like a girl's hair. I felt an unusual love for him, as if he were my own child.

As for me—I was the one in the middle, with three older siblings and three younger ones. They say middle children can often be troubled, but for me, it only made me feel more sheltered and constantly surrounded by love. The younger kids looked up to me; the older ones accepted me. I learned about the world from my older siblings and protected and cared for the younger ones. In a large family, your nature has a lot to do with how you find your place. I always aimed to please. Not a day went by when my parents didn't say, "Leah, you're such a blessing."

That may have been because they felt so thankful that I was alive at all. I had started life as a sickly child, battling a series of illnesses that—in that era before penicillin—could easily have killed me. When Father would travel to conferences or for his studies, he would visit the tombs of legendary rabbis, and when he met great sages, he would ask them to say a prayer for my health. One of the rabbis was married to a woman named Bracha. So after the rabbi said a prayer for me, my parents added Bracha to my name, and I became Bracha Leah. Another had a wife named Hinde. So I became Bracha Hinde Leah—a lot of names for such a little girl!

At two and a half, I was so ill with pneumonia that the doctor told Mother just to take me home; I wasn't going to make it. I was in such dire health that Father arranged a minyan—ten men who came to the house to pray for my health. One of his rabbis sent a messenger with a gift: a pair of earrings, each with three turquoise stones—one for each of my Hebrew names. The rabbi had said a blessing over the earrings. And it worked. When Mother put them on my ears, I opened my eyes.

"Can I get some water?" I asked her. "I'm thirsty."

Mother always told me to hold on to those earrings; they had given me life.

Whatever the reason, my parents showered me with what always felt like an overabundance of love. One Friday night when I was nine or ten, there were 13 people around the Shabbat table—the nine of us, some Talmud students, a stray bachelor or widow. Just as we were all starting into the first course, the fish, I suddenly felt a sharp pain in my throat. In my rush I hadn't removed all the bones from the carp, and a tiny sliver of a bone had become lodged in my throat. For a second, I felt like I couldn't breathe. Everyone stopped eating and talking for a moment while I sat there, turning pale. Mother gave me a firm pat on the back, but that didn't help. Father offered me water, but I just coughed. Finally, he stood up.

"Enough," said Father. "Let's go to the doctor."

Dr. Krajnik lived three blocks away and it was Shabbat, so we all knew that he would be doing just what we were doing: eating Shabbat dinner. Father got me up, and with my parents I started walking out, when I saw that everyone at the table was standing up, looks of alarm on their faces. The whole army—all 13 of us—headed out of the dining room, out the door and down the street.

This is serious, I thought. *Everyone's following me.*

We got only half a block or so before, suddenly, I started coughing again and somehow the bone became dislodged. I could breathe. I felt immediately relieved.

"I'm okay now," I told Father.

He put his arm on my shoulder, then announced to the crowd: "Okay, turn around, she's alright!" The whole party made an about-face and marched home to continue with dinner.

That night stayed with me for years, not so much because of the discomfort I felt, but because of the love I felt. Even amid what turned out to be a minor medical emergency, I had 12 people by my side. And that was how I went through my childhood: knowing that I was never alone, that I always had many others to look out for me.

I, in turn, did my share of looking out for others. It was my nature—undoubtedly a quality instilled in me by both my parents. Every day they told me how proud they were of me. Hearing that—and knowing they meant it—made me feel motivated to be even better. My parents made me feel as if I could accomplish anything.

I needed that, because I was always small—determined, but tiny. When I was six, I was the size of a four-year-old. I was very self-conscious and children would make fun of me for my diminutive size. On one of my first days at school, I tried to enter the school building but was too short to reach the door handle! I stood there on my tiptoes, trying to no avail, until finally some bigger kids came and—trying not to call attention to myself—I snuck in behind them.

Despite my size—or maybe because of it—I tried to be helpful to everyone around me. In school I always sat in the front row; I wanted to be able to see everything, but I also wanted to contribute. If the teacher would drop a pencil, I would be the first to run and pick it up. I always wanted to please.

I had a lot of friends. One of my best friends was Klari Korpner, who lived across the street from me with her five siblings. Her father was a shoe designer. When Klari was young, her mother had died in childbirth. The baby had lived and then Mr. Korpner married his wife's sister.

In school I felt happy that girls always wanted to sit with me and when we lined up for recess, I never had to look for a partner. But my parents taught me to set an example by reaching out to the less popular kids and offering to play with them. If I had ten children waiting to play with me, I would find the one who didn't have anyone. For lunch, Mother would pack me delicious meals with salami or cheese sandwiches or fresh fruit, and I would find the poor girl who had nothing but an apple. "I have so much today and I'm so little," I would say. That was just my nature.

That is not to say that I didn't know how to look out for myself. I had street smarts and common sense. I was always two steps ahead. I was in a scout group we called Cserkesz, and God gave me a sharp, vivid memory. I could read something once and memorize it. In school I got good grades without much effort.

There was only one time I remember getting into trouble—and that was a case of guilt by association. One Friday afternoon when I was eight, Mother sent my younger brother Sandor (we used his Hebrew name, Shaya) to Mr. Katzburg's nearby store to get a last minute item—the matches she needed to light the candles at the beginning of Shabbat. It was almost time to light the candles and he hadn't returned, so Mother sent me to search for him.

I found him on the steps in front of the grocery.

"Shaya," I said. "What are you doing? It's almost Shabbat! Mother is looking everywhere for you!"

"Shhhh!" whispered Shaya, who was six. "I found a pango"—a coin worth about a dollar, a lot of money for a kid in those days. "I'm going to sit on it and wait until the store closes so I can keep it."

"You should have given it to Mr. Katzburg," I told him.

"Finders keepers," he said. "It's mine."

I waited with him and after the last customer left, Mr. Katzburg pulled down the iron grate to lock up for Shabbat. Noticing us loitering there, he gestured for us to move. "Get out! Get out!" he said. "It's almost Shabbat!"

Shaya made sure nobody was looking, then picked up the coin he had been sitting on and we walked home.

When we got there, everyone was cleaning up and getting ready to head to the synagogue. Shaya hid the coin, thinking he was home free. But then Father looked at the two of us.

"Where were you?" he asked.

I wasn't one to hide the truth. So I told him. He was furious.

"On Sunday, the minute that store opens, you'll return the coin," Father demanded.

Shaya was insistent: "Finders keepers."

Father was firm. "Maybe someone needs that pango more than you do," he said.

We were both punished. Father sent me to the corner. I began to protest, but then just cried in embarrassment. My feelings were so hurt. Everybody else in the family was moving about, getting cleaned up for Shabbat, changing into nice clothing, and there I stood in my everyday skirt and top, in the corner of the living room. I cried and cried until more than an hour later, when Father and my brothers returned from the synagogue.

After that, Mother always told Father: "Don't punish Eva. If she starts crying, she doesn't know how to stop."

She didn't have to worry. I rarely gave my parents trouble. Father always trained us to be polite and respectful and to get along. He said he would have felt wrong delivering his sermons if his children weren't setting the shining example for the community. That was our way of life. We greeted everyone. We tried to get along. And if we didn't, they did not need to punish us; Mother or Father would give us a look and we knew we were out of line. That did it. Sometimes I felt that if they had spanked me, it would have been easier than the feeling of embarrassment I could feel when my father gave me that look. The worst punishment was confinement in the corner—or being forbidden from going to a movie or listening to the radio. But I knew what was right and what was wrong and I always did the right thing.

I think Father knew that. I always felt a special connection with my father—an unusual bond that almost transcended our father-daugther relationship. It was almost as if we were soul mates.

Father and I shared a passion for sweets—particularly lemon and chocolate wafers. When he traveled he would bring me some, but never gave them to me in front of the other children. He would put the wafers next to his *siddur,* his prayer book. I would take a handkerchief and sneak the cookie outside to enjoy it. He didn't have enough to share with all seven of us, and he didn't want to hurt anyone's feelings.

He was a wonderful, entertaining storyteller. On Friday nights and Saturday afternoons, he would gather all of us around his chair and tell stories from the Torah, trying to fill us up with Jewish values. His message was always the same.

"When you get up in the morning," Father would say, "look in the mirror and ask yourself how you can help somebody else."

One Friday night, in a spiritual mood, he taught us the saying from the Talmud: "If you save one life, it is as if you have saved the entire world."

He taught us how there were many ways to save a life—by giving *tzedaka* (charity) by doing good deeds—simply by always finding ways to help others. But he told us the Talmud meant it literally, too: If you can save a person's life, you should jump at the chance.

Father was a peacemaker. When there was tension, he scolded us to help each other: not harm each other. "All Jews are responsible for one another." And he would quote Hillel: "If I am not for myself, who will be for me? And if I am only for myself, what am I?" Those were sacred words that went into my bloodstream. I didn't have to write them down. It came from Father, so I cherished it. He said it, and I retained it. And he took note of that.

"Eva," he would say. "No one can take knowledge from you."

When I was 10, the teacher assigned us to write a paper on the character we most wanted to emulate in our lives. Most of the girls picked their mothers; that was simply the culture we lived in. But I wrote about my father. I just idolized him because of how fair he was, how decent he was. I thought: "This is how a human being should be." I wanted people someday to love me just the way they loved him.

And how they loved him! I would watch as he walked down the streets of Putnok. He wore a black yarmulke and, on top of that, a tall black hat. As he made his way through town, Father would tip his hat to greet people. As he went, step-by-step, he could barely put his hat back on because he had so many people to greet. He was respectful and kind and compassionate and wise. He spoke six languages. He was handsome and he had a great sense of humor. People would come to him to share their dreams. He would analyze them and try to decipher the meaning.

In synagogue, he gave inspiring sermons quoting the Torah portion we read each week. He would preach about getting along, about peace in the world. He'd help us pray for good health, tell us to give *tzedaka*. He'd tell us to pray for the weather, since Hungary was an agricultural country. (Father would practice his sermons at home, and sometimes we would offer critiques and pointers.) His words were always uplifting and filled with hope and encouragement. Those talks and his example gave me a faith and a spirituality that stayed with me for the rest of my life.

And in Putnok he earned great respect. The community provided us with our house and my parents never saw a bill. Father never took public transportation. Someone always picked him up. (The entire town had perhaps fifteen automobiles—owned by doctors and lawyers and driven by chauffeurs—and most of us got around on bicycles.) We never had doctor bills; if someone in the rabbi's family was sick, the care was free. When we bought textiles, we always had a discount. It wasn't out of pity—it was respect. People considered it an honor that the rabbi and his family would patronize a store. And people in the community didn't consider it proper for the rabbi to shop at the same time as everyone else. In the middle of the day, stores would close; that was when Father would shop. Two or three times a year, when it was time for new shoes for us kids, we would wait until lunch time, and Father would bring all of us. They would fit us with shoes. But they didn't charge. Father would pull out his money for four pairs and they would charge him for one. There was no discussion. *"Yashar koach,"* the owner would say—Congratulations. The same thing happened when we shopped for winter coats or summer clothes or raincoats.

Mother contributed in her own way. She was constantly involved in acts of charity. Every day she would wake up early, and if someone in the community was sick, she would make a pot of soup and deliver it—often anonymously. Mother would ring the doorbell, then put down the pots and pans and run off. She always taught us that it's best when you help someone not to let the person know you are helping.

Like most women in Europe of that era, she ran the home—with help from a couple of household helpers who would go with her to the open-air market to shop a couple of times a week. She was a great cook, preparing two or three kinds of meat in every meal: beef, chicken, turkey. In the summer we would eat more fish; the fishermen's wives would arrive at our door on Friday mornings with fish so fresh from the river that sometimes they were still moving!

She made flavorful, savory soups every day that would fill the house with powerful, wonderful aromas: noodles, rice, cabbage, chicken paprikash. She baked all of our bread, making the dough from scratch and then, after it rose, taking it to the neighborhood baker who would bake the bread in his oven.

She organized the women's group for the Jewish community, but then she turned over the leadership to another woman. After all, she had seven children to raise and Putnok had no restaurant serving take-out. Mother was responsible for breakfast, lunch and dinner for nine people every day.

So while Father dispensed the deep wisdom of the Jewish tradition, Mother focused on more practical matters. She kept a tidy, spotless, organized house and she kept us children neat and clean. She taught us how to clean our rooms and how to wash our hair and clean our nails.

"Wherever you are, take a bath every day and always stay clean," she would tell me. She had a friend who was a nurse and she would tell us that the nurses would check and see whether patients in the hospital were wearing clean underwear and how clean their ears were. I never wanted to be made fun of, so I listened to Mother and kept myself clean and neat.

Mother routinely shared the same piece of advice: "Whenever you leave the house, always have a safety pin and a *filler"* — the equivalent of a dime — in case of an emergency. If you tripped and fell and your bra came loose, you could fix it with the safety pin; you didn't want to be embarrassed. And one other thing: "Don't forget the house key!"

It was good advice, but it was hardly necessary in the little town of Putnok, where we didn't lock our doors and there was always a familiar adult around in case anything went awry. My parents shielded us from grief. Though, as rabbi, Father regularly visited people in the hospital and routinely officiated at funerals, I never went to the hospital and never once went to a funeral. I never saw a dead body. Father simply didn't want to expose us to horrible, gruesome situations. The violence I experienced in my early years was confined to occasional rumors of a fistfight between two boys, with injuries limited to a bloody nose or two.

LIFE FELT SAFE AND COMFORTABLE and unthreatening in every way — all the more so because of the strong religious traditions that guided our lives and dictated the pace and texture of our days, our weeks and our seasons. From early childhood, I learned the prayers that acknowledged God's active presence at every turn in our lives. When I woke up in the morning, I would do the traditional ritual of washing my hands, first thing. I would say *Modeh Ani,* the morning's first prayer. I learned a prayer for everything I ate, everything I did. Every time I put on a new piece of clothing, there was a blessing. In our Orthodox world, the boys were expected to delve into the deeper texts but less was expected of the girls. At dinner, Father would tell us,

"Say a *bracha*" — a blessing. And he would quiz us: What would you say for bread? What would you say when you hear thunder? There was a *bracha* for everything. We had to know because we would be teaching our children some day.

Though our Jewish education was limited, Jewish tradition made its way into the most intimate parts of our lives. Growing up, I never had a boyfriend, since in religious families the eldest daughter always dated and married first. Even for a second daughter to marry first would have been a scandal. I had two girls in front of me in line, so when suitors came, I had to hide out of sight. I had friends who were boys, but we would socialize in groups.

More than that, Shabbat was the center of our religious lives. After Mother lit the candles on Friday night, Father would take the boys to shul, we girls would pray at home, and then Mother would ask us about what happened that week in school. When the men returned, Father would make Kiddush over the wine and we would sing *zemirahs*, festive Shabbat songs. The girls didn't sing; we were in the background. After dinner, we girls would help Mother clean up and Father would take the boys and study that week's Torah portion.

The whole mood of the house was different on Shabbat. The lights were turned low. We didn't turn on the heat. All the food was prepared in advance. On Friday, Mother would place the *cholent*—the bean and barley stew—in an oven to cook slowly and we would eat it Saturday at lunch. On Shabbat afternoon, Father would take a nap for two hours or so on a divan in the living room, then in the afternoon he would go back to shul and neighbors would drop by to visit. (Mother rarely went to shul. Once a month, on Rosh Chodesh—the first day of the month—women would go.)

Those rituals were repeated over and over, week after week, as they had been for decades and centuries before us. We didn't tire of them. They were a way of life.

And so were the holidays. For Passover, the whole family helped to clean the house for more than a week. We scoured the floors and closets to be sure there wasn't a crumb of *chametz*—leavened bread. We aired out mattresses and brought in a special set of dishes from the attic. It was hard work, but it was a nice change. We all took naps the afternoon before the Seder, the festive Passover feast. All of Father's Talmud students would come and we stayed up past midnight listening to Father explain everything and waiting for Elijah, the prophet who tradition says visits every Passover Seder.

For Sukkot, we would build a *sukkah*—a temporary booth—behind the house, and the children would decorate it with artwork and fruit hanging from the ceiling. Father would sleep in the sukkah that week. Sometimes it would rain, but he didn't mind.

In the summer at Tisha b'Av—the commemoration of the destruction of the Temple in Jerusalem 2000 years before—I watched my mother cry, sitting in mourning on a low stool in Putnok, Hungary, to mourn a tragedy which had occurred two millennia earlier, more than a thousand miles away.

It was all vivid and deep—the holidays gave structure to our time and meaning to our days and weeks and months.

Yet as much as our lives were steeped in Judaism and Jewish practice, I didn't live in a closed world. We mixed freely and openly with Putnok's Christians.

Father had close and cordial relationships with the Protestant minister and the Catholic priest, who even invited him to deliver a sermon in the hall adjacent to the church, a huge, cavernous structure on the town square, next to city hall. And because of his position in the community, he was on close terms with the sheriff and most of the town officials.

My parents were both friendly with two nuns, middle-aged women we called Sister Anne and Sister Paula. They visited the house often to collect for the church or a Catholic orphanage. Father always gave them a donation and even sent around a *pushke*—a collection jar—at the synagogue to gather a donation from the congregation. Mother would welcome them into the house and serve tea and cookies. It felt like an honor to have these holy women in their habits sitting in our salon.

At Passover, when we had our Seders, my parents always invited gentiles. And at Christmas, our Christian friends would invite us to celebrate with them. When groups would come singing Christmas carols outside our home, Father let me go along to join in the beautiful music. "You shouldn't say 'Yeshua,' " he would tell me, using the Hebrew name for Jesus. "But just sing with the rest of them." I did and I loved being part of that beautiful, festive time of year.

We were close friends with our next-door neighbors, an affluent Catholic farming family named Toth. The Toths raised cows and horses and chickens. Mother often bought food from them; it was more convenient than going to the open-air market. There were four children: Irene, who was my age, and her brothers Laszlo, Pista, and Janchi. Our kitchen window faced their garden and we had constant interaction with their family.

And though I was certainly aware of anti-semitism, my experience of it was very limited. Once in a while we would hear that peasant boys had accosted an elderly Jewish man outside the synagogue and stolen his *siddur* or his *tallis*—the ritual prayer shawl worn by Jewish men. The incidents were isolated and they weren't taken seriously by Father and the community or by the secular authorities. Father would talk it over with the sheriff and they would agree that the perpetrators were simply bored children with nothing better to do. Father figured if he told the sheriff maybe he would pick up the youths, but the sheriff never did.

Sometimes bullies would pick fights with Jewish boys. I would hear them say "Dirty Jew" or "Stinking Jew." But we were used to it. They would fight. Later, the Jewish boys would find ways to get even. It wasn't deep anti-semitism. There wasn't damage to the synagogue or our homes. It was mostly just verbal abuse—infrequent, isolated, and not really part of our daily lives.

It certainly never felt like anything that would affect my life. When I thought about my future, I didn't dream much beyond Putnok. I just wanted to get married and be a mother. That was every girl's plan. I didn't have a profession. My two older sisters learned to sew, and we had cousins who owned a hat shop in another city. Mother suggested occasionally that I learn to make hats. A lot of religious Jewish girls learned to make *sheitls*—the wigs Orthodox women wore to cover their hair. I didn't want to mess with hair. I just liked people—and books. As a child I would play library, and I thought perhaps some day I would become a librarian. I had the patience and the interest.

I learned about the rest of the world from radio broadcasts or newsreels at the theater. Father subscribed to Jewish publications from other parts of Europe. I had read at the library about faraway places like California, where they had the most wonderful lemons and oranges. But my dreams never took me beyond the beautiful, pastoral town that had embraced my family so warmly, the place where my father couldn't walk down the street without being greeted by somebody, the place where I felt safe and loved and protected.

If we questioned the ways of the world, Father would say: "It's God's will. Accept it." It was a way of life and I thought I would live and die in Putnok. Or maybe, if I married a boy from another city in Hungary, I would move there. But I never wanted to leave Hungary. I never thought I would live anywhere else.

I hardly sensed that soon the world would have other plans for me.

2

'The World Is On Fire'

SUDDENLY, ALMOST OVERNIGHT, everything changed. In my fourteenth year, the peaceful, safe town of my childhood became filled with unimaginable dangers.

I had a scooter I loved to ride around the neighborhood. One day as I sped down a street with Sandor, who was on his bike, an unfamiliar voice stopped me. I looked up to see a tough looking boy, no more than 12 or 13. I paused and looked him over. I didn't recognize him and I knew he was not Jewish.

"Get off your scooter!" he said.

I hesitated. It was my favorite toy. And what right did he have to it? But there was nothing I could do. No one was there to protect us. Haltingly, I handed over my beloved plaything, and the boy sped off, a delighted grin on his face. I stood there, alone, in tears, and then slowly made my way home on foot.

"Mom," I said when I returned. "A boy took my scooter!"

Mother was sympathetic, trying to reassure me. But I had the clear impression that my parents weren't going to try to get my scooter back. It was a lost cause. "As long as you didn't get hurt," she said. "That's the important thing."

The truth was that I was in deep pain—and not only for the loss of my scooter. This wasn't simply an isolated case of one wayward child. In the late 1930s, as I entered adolescence, the darkness enveloping Europe had begun reaching into even our small, isolated town. For as long as I could remember, we Jews had been Hungarians with equal standing. But that was changing. The isolated anti-Jewish incidents of my youth had come to be more and more a part of our lives, even for children. And our gentile neighbors—previously friendly or at worst benignly aloof—had come under the grips of this irrational hatred.

I didn't know why it was happening, but this much I understood: The boy had made me his target because he knew I was Jewish. And nobody was going to stop a crime against a Jew.

Still, Mother tried to reassure me.

"Times will change," she said. "You'll get another scooter—a newer and better one."

Somehow I didn't believe her. Even at my young age, I had an awareness of what was going on elsewhere in the world—how the Nazis had taken over parts of Europe and how their policies had specifically focused on persecuting Jews. As early as 1938, Hungary began passing laws persecuting Jews and almost daily we heard about incidents of anti-Semitism. Hoodlums would seek out Jewish men and manhandle them. Thugs would pull Jews off trains and rough them up and take their wallets or their watches. No one stopped them. They went unpunished.

Almost daily, graffiti appeared on Jewish homes and on the shul: *Dirty Jew. Drop Dead Jew. Stinking Jew.* Where had this intense hatred come from? One incident escalated into many. We took soap and water and brushes and cleaned off the words and tried to go on with life. In the Jewish cemetery, vandals went on rampages, writing graffiti and breaking headstones. Father would organize for the Jewish community to clean up. When it happened again, we cleaned up again.

Looking back, people wonder why we didn't do anything to stop it. Why didn't the Jews organize—just as they had in education and business—and defend themselves? Why didn't we fight it?

We certainly tried. Father spent hour after hour drafting letters—to rabbis in Budapest, to the government—asking for help. He appealed to the Catholic priest, but the priest did nothing. He explained that these matters were beyond his control. It was the law of the land.

Father spent day after day drafting letters of protest to the town officials:

"Enough is enough! We're Hungarian citizens."

"I'm a patriot. I need to protect my family."

"Why are you doing this to me?"

He never got an answer. Raising questions did no good. When we would ask, "What was the crime we committed?" The answer was simple: "You're a Jew."

With persecution so rampant, why didn't we try to flee the country when we had the chance? A few Jews left in the 1930s for Palestine. But in our community that wasn't encouraged. We were Orthodox; most of the Jews settling Palestine were secular. On kibbutzim, men and women lived together, worked side by side, and traditional practice was less important than the pioneering spirit of building, farming and developing the homeland. In the 1930s, our friend Yankel Weisz, the Hebrew-school teacher, nearly lost his position because he had let his oldest son move to Palestine. Religious Jews certainly supported building the Jewish state, but the leaders encouraged sending money to buy land—not sending people to settle it.

So Father would never let any of us go. A cousin suggested that Andor move there, since he could get work as a cantor. But Father simply wouldn't allow his son to be so far away.

Nor was there much discussion of trying to move anywhere else. I did have one uncle, Morris Klein from Hajdúszoboszló who fled to the United States in the 1930s, jumping on a ship and working his way there. He arrived with no money and settled in Detroit. But that was the exception. Most middle class people simply didn't leave Hungary.

Of course, the real problem at that point wasn't an inability to move. It was a lack of imagination. Human nature is such that, until the noose is around your neck, you just don't believe anything bad could happen to you. We read in the newspapers about Adolf Hitler and anti-Semitism. We knew the Germans had occupied Austria and Czechoslovakia, whose border was less than a kilometer from Putnok.

(My parents wrote letters to cousins in both countries expressing concern—and never heard back.) When we heard reports about whole families and communities being forced from their homes, we simply didn't believe them.

We could not imagine things could be that bad and that people wouldn't do anything about it—that the leaders of the free world could let this happen.

"They're totally exaggerated," Father would say of the reports. "Some of it is true, but a lot of it is just politics and propaganda."

With time, and in horrifying ways, the stories we had been hearing became increasingly real.

One haunting, ominous sound punctuated my life in those years and always brought with it news of bad things to come. Each morning around 10 a.m., a messenger sent by city hall would appear on central street corners and begin beating a drum. The *rat-a-tat-tat* went on for five or ten minutes, warning people that he was about the make an announcement. And then, when dozens or even hundreds of people— young, old, Jewish, gentile—had run from their homes and businesses and gathered around, he began to announce the latest edicts against the Jews. I stood there, day after day, eyes glued to this man in his jacket with brass buttons and his shielded hat, dreading what would come out of his mouth—the declarations, the punishments that would follow for those who didn't obey them. The herald would travel from corner to corner, beating his drum and repeating the same awful news. And he always finished with the same bitter words: "For anyone who doesn't follow these orders, there will be severe consequences."

That was how we got the news that made our lives more difficult and miserable by the day.

The government piled on the restrictions, issuing decrees in such rapid succession that we could hardly keep up with them. First the Hungarian government stripped Jews of their positions within its ranks, from the highest diplomat to the lowliest clerk. Universities were required to expel Jews. Marriages between Jews and gentiles were forbidden. Jews lost their business licenses and had to turn over their operations to gentile employees.

For a girl in her early teens, it was hard to take it all in. Over and over, I heard Father say the same thing: "The world is on fire, and we're in the middle of it. We're burning. And there's no way out."

The government restricted our movement. There were curfews at night and we couldn't shop until after 10 in the morning, when practically all of the fresh goods—bread, milk, eggs—had already been sold. And there were strict limits on how much Jewish families could buy. Flour, matches, light bulbs—they rationed all of it. And the sheriff's deputies—without notice and without a search warrant—would barge into the homes of wealthy Jewish families to make sure they weren't hoarding anything. They would scour the basements and attics and pantries to be sure nothing was in excess.

If they found excessive quantities—of luxuries like leather and jewelry or of staples like sugar and flour—the authorities would confiscate everything, then arrest the head of the household. The men were dragged from their homes and sent to internment camps. Their families would hear nothing for weeks and months. And there was no way to find out what had become of the men.

It seemed no Jew was exempt. It didn't matter how old you were, or how much money you had, or how powerful you had been before. In fact, the first man taken from Putnok was a man named Jacob Birinbaum, a wealthy textile manufacturer who had ten or eleven children. I heard that the sheriff had come and checked his attic. Then they brought a wagon and removed everything considered surplus. His wife, in tears, pleaded with the sheriff.

"Take whatever you want," she said. "But please don't take my husband."

They had no mercy. They took Mr. Birinbaum and several of the older sons.

I heard that, and trembled. It didn't make sense. I wondered what had Mr. Birinbaum done wrong to deserve such punishment?

All we knew was that the men were being taken to labor camps. We didn't know where—or what they were doing.

But we had a clue. As it happened, one of the forced-labor camps the government had established was right in Putnok. Hundreds of men from other cities were being brought there. (None of them were from nearby. The government was intentionally moving men from their hometowns in an effort to break up families and rob people of their dignity.) It was in a military base across the river from where we lived. Sometimes the Jewish men there were able to get permission to leave for Shabbat and we would host them for meals and I heard them tell my parents about what happened in the camp. They slept in military barracks but the men running the camps didn't treat them like members of the Hungarian military. They wore civilian clothes and heavy boots and did hard labor all day.

With that frightening reality before us, I took comfort in one thing: They weren't going to take my father. After all, he was a decorated war hero. And he had a close friendship with the sheriff. Besides that, we weren't hoarding any rationed foods or other materials. We weren't considered suspect, so the deputies never came to search our house.

Then, in the fall of 1940, a letter arrived with Father's name on it. He opened the envelope and sat in stunned silence.

"It must be a mistake," he said.

"What is it?" Mother asked.

"This can't be right," said Father.

The letter was an official government notice. It ordered Father to report to the camp in the city of Hatvan, about 100 miles away, immediately. He sat in stunned silence. Mother began to cry. I knew it was an error. They simply would not have called my father, a respected elder of the community, to a work camp. It was all so unreal.

"They couldn't have meant to send this," he said. "But I'll go and straighten this out."

By then we had seen so many men disappear—leaving no idea of where they were or when they might return—that it was difficult to believe he could do anything to stand up for himself. Mother was beside herself. But she helped him prepare for the journey, baking him some Danish pastry, and preparing some chicken for him—enough food to last a day. Father put the food in a small suitcase with his *tallis* (his prayer shawl), and the *tefillin* he wore when he prayed on week-day mornings. Standing in the doorway to leave, he gave us each a kiss and reassured us again.

"This was all a mistake," he said. "I'll be back before you know it." I stood with Mother and watched him head down the street toward the train station. And then we waited, not knowing when—or if—we'd see him again.

Then came a minor miracle. That Friday afternoon, just two days after he had left, the door opened, and in walked a man. It took me a minute to realize it was Father. He looked so odd and different. The Hungarians had let him go, but not before they had shaved his thick, dark beard and his *payes*, the curly sidelocks Orthodox men wore. They had done it to humiliate him. It was the first time in my 13 years I had ever seen his full, round, beautiful face.

"It's still me," he said. "I just look *goyish*."

We were jubilant to see him and I secretly thanked God for looking out for my father. Still, thrilled as I was to see him, it upset me to see him this way, somehow diminished and violated by the mere act of a shave.

With all the changes around us, we also experienced changes within our household. Andor, my oldest brother, had left Putnok in 1938 to become cantor of a synagogue in Budapest. He was only 17 when he started. At first, the shul's president was concerned about hiring a bachelor for such an important position. He insisted that Andor get married, and he employed the local matchmakers to find him a bride. Everyone they brought was five or six years older than Andor, and when Mother heard this, she was horrified. In the end, the shul gave in—they wanted a cantor—and let him take the position even without a wife.

With all of the new forms of persecution we were experiencing, many Jews were moving to Budapest, where the restrictions weren't being felt as much. Jews could still work and because of the larger population, the Jews could blend in more with the general populace and had much more freedom. Besides that, there was more work opportunity and better pay. My two older sisters, Aranka and Irene, were talented seamstresses. They had learned to embroider and knit. Aranka could make men's shirts, and Irene knew how to make dresses. Two of the Jewish textile manufacturers in Putnok had factories in Budapest, so my sisters were able to secure jobs there. A year later, Sandor, who was two years younger than I, joined them. He was learning a trade, making silver jewelry by day and studying in a yeshiva at night. Sometimes they would return for Jewish holidays and Sandor would bring me a silver bracelet or ring. I was delighted.

With the four of them in Budapest, that left just five of us at home: Father, Mother, me, Valerie and Viktor. Suddenly, I went from being the middle child to being the oldest. It made me feel special, and also I took on more responsibilities for the family. One morning the drummer on the corner's announcement was that Jewish families could no longer employ gentiles as household employees. That meant Mother had to let go Terry and Molly, the two women who had worked for our family for so long, helping to raise us and keep the house running. I spent more of my time doing those chores: cooking, washing dishes, and taking care of the young children.

In the midst of all this, we got a glimpse of what was happening in the rest of Europe. It happened on the holiday of Simchat Torah, in the fall of 1942. When Father returned from services, he told us a messenger from city hall had arrived at the synagogue during services that morning and handed a note to the *shames*, the shul's caretaker, who brought it to Father. The message said that a group of Czechoslovakian Jews would be passing through Putnok that day.

"Let's go meet them and take them some food," Father said.

I didn't understand what they were doing. Where were they going? Why had they come?

But we had plenty of food prepared for the holidays, so I helped Mother pack it up: stuffed cabbage, chicken, duck, goose—everything we could. And we gathered several other Jewish families and rushed to the town square to meet these strangers.

Along they came, about 200 of them. They weren't impoverished refugees. These were wealthy people—doctors, lawyers, businessmen—and it showed. They carried elegant suitcases. Some of the women wore furs. They spoke Hungarian and Yiddish and they told us their stories. The Germans had deported all of the Jews from Czechoslovakia, from the smallest villages to the largest cities. They told us they were the last ones left. It was hard to fathom, but these people had somehow avoided being deported—probably by using their wealth to bribe their way out—and made their way to the border village of Bánréve, just two kilometers from Putnok. From there, they had crossed the border and made their way to Putnok, where they could catch a train for Budapest, where they hoped to find new lives.

It was all too much to take in. It was the first time I had ever heard the word "deportation." It was a foreign concept, the idea that you could be sent from your own country to some unknown place. It was difficult to believe what they were telling us: Whole communities had been forced into ghettos and then taken away in trains and never heard from again. Where had they gone? The Czech visitors couldn't tell us, because they themselves didn't know. The Germans and Czechs had driven them from their homes, but they escaped with whatever they could: cash, jewelry, the clothes on their backs.

We pitied them, but even after that, I didn't feel it was a warning for us—not one that we could hear. We didn't think our turn would come. The Czechs reassured us: "Hungary is such a liberal country," they said. "It would never collaborate with the Germans." That gave us hope.

Yet we never knew what would happen next. Soon we got word that the government had ordered Andor, my oldest brother, to report for forced labor at a town called Koszeg. Abruptly, he had to leave the synagogue in Budapest. With the bitter winter bearing down on us, Mother's immediate response to the news was to go shopping. She bought him a fur hat, a fur coat, and warm underwear to help him endure the frigid temperatures.

A few months after he reported, he got released for a few days leave and returned to Putnok, looking pale and thin. He had lost at least 20 pounds. He'd worked in the rain and snow, shoveling and do-ing construction. He told us how harshly the cruel guards had treated him.

"Look what's happened to my Yosele," said Mother.

The new clothes she had bought him were ruined, damp and covered with mold. She couldn't get them clean, so she put them in the trash and we went shopping again, picking up heavy boots, a warm coat, wool pants, thick gloves, a new hat.

He was traveling with another young man named Pal. I was just at the age when I was starting to notice boys, and I couldn't help but observe how handsome Pal was. He looked like Charles Boyer, the French movie star. Pal had been born Jewish but raised Catholic, and he was studying to be a priest. But since he had Jewish blood, the Hungarians pulled him out of seminary and sent him to forced labor. Some time later, Pal wrote me a postcard. (Father didn't want me to see it, lest I start an affair with a priest, but Mother let me look.) He said he'd never forget me and when the war was over, he hoped to get to know me better. With all that was going on around me, it was a pleasant diversion!

Andor stayed long enough to take a warm bath and have a home-cooked meal and then he departed to return to the labor camp.

We received letters from Andor regularly—never more than a few words: "I am fine. I miss all of you." But we were never certain how he was really faring.

Just as Andor had been taken, men were being forced from their homes daily. Besides the scattered reports, we had no idea where they were taken. We all feared the worst. Many of them were shipped to Ukraine, where word had it there was a need for laborers. Lawyers, doctors, wealthy businessmen—there were no exceptions—men who had never done any physical labor suddenly found themselves toiling at the hands of brutal guards. Some tried to bribe the guards, but that rarely worked.

Sometimes our worst fears were confirmed. The Jewish newspaper we got every weekend carried seemingly endless lists of the names of men who had died. (We learned later they had frozen to death or died from being tortured or beaten by guards.)

With all of the men being taken, our Jewish community became a place with almost no young men. I wandered in a world of old men, women, grandmothers and us children. The life I had known felt dark and destroyed. The city felt half dead. Yet I also knew how lucky I was; my father was one of the few able-bodied Jewish men still at home.

Many other families weren't as lucky. They felt vulnerable and unprotected, and Father spent much of his time bringing comfort and words of hope to those who remained. He went from house to house, visiting, attending to the sick, and trying his best to spread hope.

"We still have our children," he reassured them. "The men will come home." In the meantime, he urged us to take care of each other.

Those who still had the strength still went to shul, where Father, in his talks, would acknowledge the difficult times we were going through, but he urged us all to have faith that we would endure this crisis.

"The Jewish people have suffered in the past," he would say. "Look what happened in Egypt." On Shavuot, he would say, "We're God's chosen people. The time will come." He encouraged us to be more united, to be more observant. "God is telling us we have to change," he would say.

Father's clear message was that all of this was happening for a reason, and that God would give us strength to cope with it. "This is the history of our people. Look at how our ancestors suffered. Now it's our turn. The Jewish people will survive and prevail. It's going to turn for the better. We just have to have faith in God and pray, and not question God's will."

Mostly he tried to sow hope. How much worse could it get?

"They'll get tired of this," he would say. "Someone will see that this isn't justice, and things will turn around for the better."

Yet I'm sure that he carried his own fears. Children always think their mother and ather will protect them. Yet I knew deep down that my parents were every bit as scared as I was.

And for good reason: Every morning, the drummer's beat would bring more bad news from the Hungarian authorities: Jews cannot go to school. Jews cannot travel between cities. As we would adjust to one set of rules, they would add another. I came to feel like an ob-

46

ject—like a machine. There was no peace. You couldn't make plans, because the new rule would stop you. I felt helpless and hopeless— we all did.

The Jewish community held a meeting to discuss what to do about education. But the law was that school had to stop. Sometimes the *melamed*—the Hebrew teacher—would gather children in the school-yard and try to have Hebrew lessons. We would visit the English teacher, Lenke Schreiber, who lived on the Synagogue yard, and she would give us assignments. We stayed home, reading books from the library and listening to the radio. We helped with chores. We played games. I did a lot of embroidery and darned socks.

Outside, as Father kept saying, the world was on fire.

The gentile Hungarians tried to embarrass us, to humiliate us, to break our spirit in any way they could. Not only did the police look the other way, they actively participated. One word that filled me with dread was *razzia*—the term for a police raid in which officers would run down the street attempting to harm as many Jewish people as possible, striking and beating whomever happened to pass by. People would come home with broken bones and bloody noses and their clothes ripped off their backs. There was no peace, not a single safe moment.

Mother, like all of the other Jewish mothers, lived in fear for her children. She cautioned us not to stir up any trouble.

"Just follow orders," she would say, "and you'll stay out of trouble."

What our parents didn't tell us was to fight back. That wasn't seen as the Jewish way. From his experience in the First World War, Father knew what it meant to fight. But at home, he told us, it was wiser to give in and avoid escalating a fight.

"If you fight, it could get worse," he would say. "Just walk away." That was the Jewish way. And following orders, he said, brought its own rewards.

I held on to my hopes. I'm sure that my parents sheltered me from a lot of things, so perhaps any hopes I had were merely illusions. If my parents worried that we risked being deported like the Czechs, they didn't share those fears with me.

"As long as we're all together, life will go on," Father would say. "It will just be a little different."

Every day, we didn't think it could get worse. We thought it would get better. We had hope and strength. We felt resilient. We just didn't think of the unthinkable.

3

Occupation

I WAS AT HOME ON A BEAUTIFUL, clear Sunday afternoon when I was startled to feel the earth shaking and I heard rumbling and shouting from outside. It was March 19, 1944. I was 16 years old. For weeks we had been hearing on the radio and newspaper that Hungary's leaders had agreed to collaborate with the Nazis. The German invasion was imminent.

That news did not fill me with fear or panic, since I had no real concept of what that might mean for my family and me. I had a strong sense of curiosity and I knew this was an important event. Knowing that the invasion was imminent, our family didn't try to flee. We stayed, waiting to see what would happen.

When the invasion arrived, I wanted to see for myself. I didn't want to hear second hand. So I ran out to the street to see what was going on. Standing on the street outside the synagogue I took in the shocking site: an endless line of vehicles—armored tanks, massive trucks, jeep after jeep. The line went on for blocks and blocks, as far as I could see forward, as far as I could see backward.

I stood in frozen silence, surveying the scene. I didn't feel a sense of danger; it was just something new and different—like the circus coming to town. I knew exactly what the Germans represented, but I thought: *This is history. This is different. Hungary is being invaded! This is an earth-shattering event!* I didn't want to be in the house. I wanted to see what it looked like to be invaded! To a teenager, this was exciting. I didn't want to communicate with the soldiers or shake their hands. I didn't want to welcome them. I just wanted to see.

As I watched, the line came to a slow halt in front of the synagogue. Men started getting out of the tanks, not aggressively, just to stretch and look around, as if they had traveled a long way and just needed to move their bodies around a bit. I had very long hair; that was the style at the time. All of us girls had hair down to our waists. As I stood at the gate of the shul, with Mother not far behind, and watched the soldiers drink their water and feel their way around, one young officer suddenly looked me in the eye.

"*Schönes longes Haar,*" the soldier said—What beautiful hair you have.

I looked away bashfully, and Mother grabbed me by the arm.

"Come inside," she said.

I followed her into the house, leaving the commotion outside. Inside, she sat me down, and then left the room. She came back with a pair of scissors. I was confused.

"What are you doing?" I asked.

"Leah, you heard what the officer said," Mother said. "You have long, beautiful hair. You don't want to call attention to yourself. It's not good for you. You could get hurt."

I had tears in my eyes as Mother cut my long, brown locks, leaving me with hair just down to my shoulders. Suddenly, I began to take in what this invasion might mean. It wasn't just exciting. It was scary.

"I want you to stay in the house," she told me.

Unable to witness the historic happenings outside, I could only imagine the events transforming my town. Suddenly I faced a new reality: I had to protect myself or I could get hurt. Other mothers were telling their daughters the same thing: Don't go outside. The German Army could harm you. Mother didn't explain exactly how, but somehow I understood.

For the first few days, not much happened. The Germans made

themselves at home in Putnok. They set up mobile kitchens and medical units. At first the Germans didn't go inside our homes or touch the synagogue.

We stayed home, but Father would come and go, reporting that things were quiet. There was no shooting. The Germans were simply awaiting their orders. As the days passed, I felt more and more anxiety simply from the long wait to see what would come next.

Then, two weeks later, the newspapers and radio—and the drummer on the corner—announced the news: Starting April 5 Jews would be required to wear yellow stars when we were in public. The order told us the specific measurements. Mother and I went to a textile store and purchased yellow materials. Mother cut the stars—one for each of the five of us still at home—following the details of the order, and sewed them onto our jackets. Some people used pins or paper clips or safety pins. I was horrified. It felt embarrassing and humiliating, being forced to display your religion on your clothing. I thought I would just never leave the house.

That first day, a Wednesday morning, Mother asked me to go to the bakery to buy some bread.

"Mother, can't I please stay home?" I begged. "I'm too ashamed to go out."

She looked at me. "The ones who made you wear the yellow star should be ashamed," she said. She told me we needed the bread, so she would come with me. We left Father at home with the younger children.

I was wearing a black flannel jacket, and Mother sewed the yellow star pinned to it over my heart. Mother wore hers on a navy sweater with gold buttons. It was a short walk to the bakery, and on the way, we had to cross a short, narrow bridge over a small pond. Just then, walking the other way came the two Catholic nuns, Sisters Paula and Anne, who had collected charity and shared tea at our house. As they neared us both glared at us, and, without warning, they spit in our faces—one on Mother, one on me. Silent, they kept walking.

I was stunned. Mother simply wiped her face. I did the same. I was crying and terrified. These were nuns. I knew they were holy women

51

and their role was to be God's messengers.

"Mother," I said. "If religious people treat us this way, I can't imagine what the rest of them will do to us."

"They'll be sorry," she said. "The day will come when they will apologize. They shouldn't have done that."

I was so taken aback I could hardly walk. But we proceeded to the bakery and got the bread. When we returned home, I immediately told Father what had happened.

"Shame on them," he said. "What a shameful thing to do."

I had thought they were religious people who would set an example—who would be respectful and supportive of us Jews. They weren't, and from that day, I realized I couldn't trust anyone. I cried for hours.

"Don't make too much of it," Mother kept saying. "We're here together, and that's what counts."

One morning the drummer announced that all girls from age 15 were to report for work the next day at a large brick factory on the edge of town. I had passed the building many times, but most of the workers were gypsies and peasants. I never dreamed I would be an employee there! We were told to be ready the next morning, wearing work clothes and durable shoes.

The next morning, the sheriff arrived at our door to get me. Mother had packed me a lunch. I walked with dozens of other girls the quarter-mile to the factory. The work was difficult and draining and mindless. For eight or ten hours a day I would pick up bricks, load them into a wheelbarrow and push them from one place to another. It was the rainy season and I slogged through the mud, feeling cold and miserable.

Each night I returned home exhausted, and Mother did her best to care for me. I had never worked so hard in my life. I put my feet up and she massaged them and let me rest, then she would feed me a hot supper. My sisters in Budapest tried to cheer me up by sending a package with a long skirt and knit stockings to keep me warm.

One afternoon the sheriff announced that the next day he would assemble all the girls outside and the town judge was going to come and talk to us. We were trembling because the judge was such a powerful person. We were frightened about what he would say to us—or do to us.

The judge arrived—he was a middle-aged man in a dark three-piece suit, shiny black shoes and a hat—and we lined up, standing at attention.

"You pigs," he said. "I'm here to tell you why you were punished and why you have to do this hard labor."

I saw one of the other girls raise her hand. It was Olga Birinbaum, a beautiful young woman in her early twenties. "Your honor," she said, "I have a question."

"Jew, you can speak," he said.

"What have we done, that we have been punished?" she asked.

His answer came with rage and venom: "You're a filthy, dirty Jew and you deserve the punishment."

We were all silent. I was terrified. He dismissed us, and we went back to work.

At the end of the day I told Mother what had happened.

"I'm so afraid," I told her.

She tried to reassure me. "Well, that's his job. I'm sure he had to do his job," she said. "But it's a horrible way to treat young girls."

Of course, it hardly mattered that we were girls or that we were young. Only one thing mattered to the Hungarians: We were Jews.

PASSOVER WAS PAINFULLY SAD. Four of my sisters and brothers weren't there. In years past we would have 20 or more people around our seder table, eating and talking until one in the morning. But now, with all the restrictions on Jews traveling, it was just the five of us. We had matzah that the Jewish community in Mishkolc had been able to ship. But Father kept the seder short, and I felt a deep sadness.

Yet never had the Passover story felt so immediate and profound. As Father read the Haggadah text about the Israelites' enslavement in Egypt I didn't need to use my imagination: Andor was in a forced labor camp; and what was the brick factory if not slavery? How could we celebrate freedom, when the authorities wouldn't let Irene and Aranka travel out of Budapest for the holiday? We didn't need to eat the bitter herbs from the seder plate to taste bitterness. I felt it in every waking moment.

"We were slaves then," Father said, "and we're slaves now."

Even Father seemed to be losing hope.

THE DRUMMER ON THE STREET CORNER kept bringing bad news, and on May 9, the most dramatic announcement came: The government was forcing all Jews to move into a holding area. Every Jew left in Putnok had to move into an area encompassing about 20 blocks. And it wasn't only the Jews. The order included anyone the Nazis considered undesirable: gypsies, Seventh-Day Adventists, Jehovah's Witnesses, disabled people, the mentally retarded—even Jews who had converted to Christianity.

Father ran a Jewish council with two elderly men and he was the liaison with the German and Hungarian authorities. So he had to bring the news. There was no escaping. City Hall was eager to provide the names and addresses of all the so-called undesirables and make sure we all moved into the ghetto. It was a horrible, frightening experience.

The authorities rounded up Jews from all the surrounding villages. There was a woman named Polonie who was married to a photographer. She had been born Jewish but converted. But she was brought in. There was a Jewish farmer in a nearby village whose daughter had married one of the gentile coachmen. It had been a scandal at the time, but the coachman had converted to Judaism. At first, this couple was forced to move to the ghetto but their young children were spared and left with the coachman's parents. But later on, the sheriff forced the grandparents to deliver the two children to be with the parents.

They ordered us to pack our possessions in no more than one small suitcase or backpack. They were confiscating everything valuable: jewelry, cash. Mother packed things to help care for the family:

clothing for the young children, dishes, toothpaste, soap, towels, blankets. I could not decide what to put in my backpack. I just didn't know what I would need the most. But I was a sentimental person, so I packed items of personal value: Father's war diary, the family album, a prayer book, and the candlesticks we used on Friday nights.

At first the ghetto included our home, so we didn't have to move—but four other families moved into our home. Each family had a room. For some of the time it got more crowded and two families shared a single room. A family would get its own corner. People stayed with their own loved ones and suffered together. Mother tried to make sure people could get privacy when they needed it. People brought their own mattresses and we took our beds apart, because they took up so much room. We put the mattresses on the floor for the elderly people, the sick, and the small. We were miserable.

Still, life went on. The men prayed together every morning. The women were busy with cooking and washing and taking care of the elderly people and the sick and small children. Everyone was helping someone. You didn't live for yourself.

I was still reporting every morning with the other girls to the brick factory every day except Sunday—even on Shabbat. I didn't have a choice. So I wasn't home much during the day, but on Sundays I was there to experience the confusion and the hardship of this heartbreaking situation. It was springtime and we had a lot of rain. People were getting colds and influenza and since we were so crammed together in such a small space, the illness would spread quickly. It seemed that everyone was coughing and sneezing and had a fever. Father was the one who was able to make contact with the outside world, and he would go to a pharmacy to get aspirin and medication for everyone. He would bring tea and honey. He would meet with city leaders, arguing for medicine and clean water. But it became more and more difficult to get any help.

The longer it went on, the more difficult it became. There wasn't room to cook hot meals. We ate jam and canned foods. Mother tried to work with other women, setting up soup kitchens, making meals to share. She was tireless, working day and night to help young and old.

Many women were pregnant and went into labor in the crowded conditions. In our home, 25 or 30 people were sharing one outhouse and there was an almost constant line. Mother was out there making sure the older people could go first. Everyone helped with pumping water from the well and carrying it inside.

There were no fights. It seems difficult to believe, but we did our best to maintain order and civility. Our lives had changed drastically and we had to share everything. But we were in it together. We took care of each other. Of course, at times, somebody would lose his temper and raise his voice. The old men would say, *"Sha! Sha! Sha!"*— Quiet!

The sheriff did his share to maintain order, too, patrolling the area to make sure things were in control. With so many people in so little space he didn't want panic to break out. It would have been difficult to control so many people.

We still had a lot of books around. And somehow we got newspapers. I read about how every city in Hungary now had a ghetto. Everywhere, the government was gathering the Jews.

It was hard on the children. There was so little to do. Valerie and Viktor were tired and frightened and didn't understand what was happening. The women would play games with them to keep them entertained. The mothers and grandmothers were holding the younger children, singing lullabies. Anyone who was able would try to keep the children occupied and quiet. "It's okay, don't be afraid," I kept hearing. "Mommy is here."

Nothing made sense. But we tried to get through each day. We had lost so much, but we still had our families together. We still had food.

And then I got a chance at life. Early one morning, our neighbor, Pista Toth, knocked at the kitchen window. Pista was Catholic and I was surprised to see him. He had come with a proposal.

"Leah," he said, calling me by my Hebrew name. "You don't have to suffer in the ghetto. I can get you out."

Pista had a plan. He told me he would bring me an army-cadet uniform and I could jump over the ghetto fence. He would take me two kilometers to the village where his grandmother lived.

"You don't have to suffer like this," he said. "You can come and pretend to be part of our family."

I didn't know what to say. I needed to take care of Mother and the children. How could I abandon my family and my fellow Jews at such a dire time? But Pista tried to convince me.

"You can wear a kerchief and fit right in. You can help with the harvest and go to church. No one will know you are a Jew."

"I can't leave my family," I told me. "Can they come, too?"

He shook his head.

"I'm sorry, Leah," he said. "I'm risking my life bringing just you. To try to bring the others would just be too dangerous."

I stood, frozen, torn between the chance he was offering and my beloved family—between life and a fate that was at best uncertain.

"Come tomorrow, Leah," Pista said. "I'll be waiting at four in the morning. No one will be looking then. You can jump over the fence and I'll take you with me."

My mother was there. I asked her what I should do, and she did not hesitate.

"Go with him," she said. "You have the right to live."

"But Mother, I can't." I told her. "Pista can't take the rest of you. I can't leave you."

"Leah, just go!" she said.

But I shook my head. "I don't want to be without you."

I thanked Pista.

"I just can't." I told him. "I can't leave them."

His expression showed he understood the difficult position I was in. But there was no more that he could do. As quickly as he had come, Pista disappeared, taking with him any hope I had of escaping whatever fate awaited me.

THE GERMANS DECIDED THEY needed the synagogue and the buildings around it for themselves. They ordered us—and the four families living under our roof—to leave. That made it seem all the more real and frightening to me.

I watched Mother take down the *mezuzahs*, the scrolls that mark the doorposts of Jewish homes, with tears in her eyes. A mezuzah is what marks a place as a blessed Jewish home. She put the mezuzah from our front door in a small clutch purse with a red marble clasp.

It was spring, but it was still chilly at night. Our home had a tall, coal-burning heater. Father picked up the heavy stove, somehow lifted it onto his shoulder and carried it by himself down the pathway through the garden toward our new temporary home. It was a cumbersome piece and he looked awkward—but also determined.

"Shloyme," Mother asked. "What are you doing?"

"My family needs heat," he said.

Watching him bear that heavy load, I cried.

"Leave me alone," he said. "I'm doing what I need to do."

We had lived in that house for nearly as long as I could remember. It was where we had joyfully danced as Father played his violin and Andor sang. It was where Mother had cooked for hundreds of Shabbat dinners, where I had played dolls with Valerie. Abruptly forced out of it, my parents were desperately trying to bring what they could with them. When Jews move from a home in normal times, they leave the mezuzahs for the next residents. It was almost as if Mother and Father were symbolically trying to bring our home with them, each by taking things I never imagined would leave our home.

We all walked out the door and through our beautiful garden and into another home, half a block away.

We moved in with the Cohen family. Mr. Cohen had been a tailor. My best friend's family was there too. Klari Korpner's father had been taken away already. She was with five of her younger siblings. The elderly, retired Hebrew teacher, Mr. Hollander, was there with his wife. The Birinbaums were there—a widow and grown children. And the Lax family—another widow with six children. Somehow we managed to make the crowded house into an adequate home.

It was horrible. I had only one source of consolation and comfort: Father was still with us, virtually the last able-bodied Jewish man left in Putnok. Over the preceding months and years, the men had all been taken. It seemed a miracle that I was still holding on to my father. As weary as he was from serving the spiritual needs of our entire decrepit community, he was still my father, and he was still there for me, every night. That was a luxury almost none of my friends had.

But I was about to lose that, too.

A sheriff's deputy arrived at our door early one afternoon. We were all home. He asked for Father.

"I have to take you to the station," the deputy said. "I'll give you 15 minutes." Father was stunned. They had assured him he would not be taken from his family. The deputy himself, who knew Father well, could barely hold back his own emotion. He explained that he'd simply received an order. Father fell in the age group of men who were to be taken. He wasn't elderly. He wasn't ill or disabled. His time was up.

Father got his backpack. Mother gave him some food. He gathered his *tallis*, his *tefillin*, packed the food. He gave us each a hug and a blessing.

"God will help all of you," he said. "Take care of each other. I'll pray for all of you."

As they left, the sheriff said he would come the next morning to escort us to the train station to say farewell.

Father was a strong man—physically and emotionally. But as he left that day, he cried. We stood in the doorway watching him go, and he kept turning around, looking back and waving. We all cried.

We were devastated. We sat in stunned silence. Finally Mother spoke, trying to reassure us.

"Don't worry about Daddy," she said. "He's a war hero. He knows how to take care of himself."

The next morning, the sheriff came and the four of us walked with him to the station. As we got closer, I started noticing the crowds of people. Hundreds of gentiles were lined up at the station, applauding and cheering, jubilant at this event: The last able-bodied Jewish man was leaving their town. I felt such agony. This town that had been such a place of comfort, the only place I could call home, was now filled with such hatred. And for what? What had Father ever done to hurt any of these people? He had given his life to nothing but lifting people's spirits and serving God. Where did this venom come from?

The sheriff guided him to the section of the train where he was to sit. We didn't even know where it was going. Mother stood there. They always spoke to each other in Yiddish, and her last words to him were in Yiddish:

"Meiyn tyere *Shloyme, luhz mich nish iber!*"—My dear Solomon, please don't leave me behind!

He left. And we cried some more.

We left the station and returned to the ghetto. I felt empty—wiped out. How can you continue in life without your father?

"We have to move on," Mother said. "He blessed us. He told us to take care of each other and that's what we're going to do. Just take care of each other and pray. And God will help."

But without Father's strength, the community and our family crumbled. What had already been difficult became even worse. There was no leader to assume Father's position running the Jewish council, so conditions deteriorated. We had no one to act as advocate—to mediate conflicts that came or to help acquire medicine. We did our best simply to survive each day. Our meager food supplies were drying up. It seemed we couldn't go on for long.

A WEEK AFTER FATHER HAD BEEN TAKEN, it was our turn to go. The sheriff walked through the ghetto with a bullhorn, announcing: "Get your luggage ready! You're leaving tomorrow!"

There were guards everywhere: inside the ghetto and just outside. They made sure that no one could escape. They also told us our destination: Diosgyor, a large city with a huge foundry that manufactured iron that was shipped all over the world. The sheriff's deputies told us we were going to work there, just as I had been working at the brick factory. I believed it, but I couldn't help but wonder: Why would they be taking grandparents and small children to work in a factory? Still, I imagined we were going to settle in Diosgyör to work in the iron factory. What other explanation could there be?

Mother packed all of our immediate needs: clothes, coloring books for the children, and food—smoked goose leg, a can of sardines, hard-boiled eggs, and some cheese. I brought things of more sentimental value: the photo album, Father's diary, the candlesticks and Kiddush cup.

With the guards watching, we quietly filed out of the house. I turned to look back, filled with sadness, and saw our cat, Cecilia, creeping along behind us, looking confused at the scene.

It was June 9, 1944. We made our way to the station. Carriages picked up the elderly and disabled. Coachmen lined up to drive them and help them get to the train. The rest of us walked. Again, hundreds of our gentile neighbors showed up at the train station. They were applauding and cheering. The town would be free of Jews. They would have it to themselves.

The sights and sounds cut into my heart like a knife. The expressions on their faces as they jumped up and down were terrifying. Parents, children, young and old—celebrating our departure as if it were a soccer championship.

I boarded the passenger train, helping Mother with Valerie and Viktor. The rhythm of the locomotive blended with the sounds of cheering. I craned my neck to watch Putnok fade in the distance, and with it, my childhood, my home, and any sense of security I had ever felt.

4

Cattle Cars

THE JOURNEY WAS JUST OVER AN HOUR. The train slowed, and out the window I saw the signs: DIOSGYÖR.

We got off the train. I helped some of the older people step out of the car. The air was hot. Mosquitoes surrounded us. We put down our ragged packs in a grassy, open space near the station. Nearby was the iron foundry, but we could see that there was no one coming in or out of the foundry. It was shut down.

"What are we doing here?" I asked Mother. But she didn't know. None of us knew.

There were hundreds of us from Putnok. But we weren't alone: The whole area was crowded with thousands of Jews from all over the region. I had never seen anything like it. In Putnok, it was an occasion if a single Jewish stranger arrived on the train, and here were thousands of Jews, throngs everywhere. I was gripped by a strange, ominous feeling: shock, uncertainty and fear all at once.

With the sun beating down on us, we stayed in the grassy area, trying to take care of ourselves. For a lavatory we had an open latrine. There was no privacy, no shower.

There was confusion and crying and shouting and screaming. Nobody had enough space. The stench was awful, and there were rats and flies. Everybody was sweating profusely. In more than one place, I saw pregnant women going into labor and midwives setting up to help them. I wondered what kind of lives these newborns could possibly face.

We had no idea how long this would go on. And I kept wondering why this was happening. Why had they taken us from our hometown to sit here in the heat in these filthy conditions?

Surely somewhere, someone knew why. But we did not. Even if we had possessed the strength to fight back, whom would we have fought? What logic were we fighting against? All was confusion.

Even in these awful conditions, our people organized themselves. A small council of Jews was working to help us communicate with each other—and with the authorities. Someone had smuggled a radio and we heard reports that Hitler's vicious first lieutenant, Adolf Eichmann, had arrived in Hungary. I had read about Eichmann and heard my parents talk about him. I had seen him in the newspaper and on newsreels and I knew what he represented. The newscasts had told us he was charged with eliminating Hungary's Jews. We saw his photograph all over the newspapers.

Perhaps these were the first clues to our fate. We were terrified. We heard that trains were waiting for us, and they were going to ship us out of Hungary. Should I believe it?

Five days after we arrived, on the morning of Tuesday, June 13, we were marched to the train station. The guards shouting in megaphones told us we were going to be leaving Hungary. "Where are we going?" people asked.

"We're taking you somewhere where workers are needed," one of the guards told us.

"How long will we be traveling?" one man asked.

"You'll find out when you get there," he said.

We didn't know if it would be a day or a week. We all had endless lists of questions. When will we see our loved ones? Can we stay together? When can we go home? They explained nothing. My imagination ran wild. It was all so new. There was one word on everybody's lips: "deportation."

They told us to take our backpacks with us. But we had subsisted those five days on jam and margarine and bread. Now, virtually nothing was left.

Thousands of people streamed into the train station in Diosgyor. Armed guards directed us to the platform, but when we got there, there were no passenger trains. We saw only cattle cars.

I thought, "This is not for people." The cars were rust colored with three painted letters: "MAV" for Magyar Allamvasutak, the Hungarian rail company. There was no seating, just a filthy wooden floor, barely adequate for animals.

I looked for windows. There were none, except for a single small opening covered with an iron screen. It didn't open. I stood in stunned silence.

The guards stood by with their machine guns, ordering us to gather our possessions and climb in.

"Get up! Get up!" they shouted. "Get going!"

We helped the older people and those who were ill. The guards forced us inside, where we lined up like sardines, elbow to elbow. There were 80 or 100 people in a single car. Most of the people in my car were from Putnok. The very elderly sat down on the floor, but the young didn't have room to sit. People sat on each other's laps, on top of each other, our breath beating down on each other. Some tried to sit on their backpacks.

In those days, people dressed up to travel, and we were all still wearing what we had set out in five mornings earlier—it seemed a lifetime ago—in Putnok. I had on a pink skirt my sister Irene had sent; she had taken a dress whose top was worn out and turned it into a skirt with straps that fit me. I wore a pink blouse with sleeves that covered my elbows—in the modest style we religious girls wore. I had on white sandals and stockings. Mother had on a navy blue dress with white polka dots, and her kerchief covering her head. Viktor was in a cute gray suit; Valerie wore a little navy dress. Here we were, in our fancy travel clothes, trying to get comfortable in a cattle car. I sat on the floor and held Viktor in my lap for comfort. Mother held Valerie.

We had no water or food. And they didn't give us any.

Suddenly, the guard slammed the door shut and we heard him secure it with an iron rod. It was dark. There was no way out.

For two days, that car would be our prison.

I noticed right away that standing next to me in the dim light was one of the most respected and religious men in Putnok, Moishe Yosef Lovy. He was probably 80 years old and had a beautiful face with a long beard. He walked with a cane. Back in Putnok, Mr. Lovy was so prominent and beloved that he was like glue, keeping all the Jews together. I tried to move over so he could sit down. He was just so restless. After a while I could tell that he had to go to the bathroom. Mother had packed bed sheets for the children. So she asked me to go into the pack and take out a sheet. Mother and I got him the bucket and held up a sheet so Mr. Lovy could have some privacy while he relieved himself. We looked away while he went. Then Mr. Lovy looked at me.

"That was a *mitzvah*," he said. "I needed to go so badly."

He was embarrassed. I thought, *If Father could see this!* And I just cried.

A young woman who had married into the Goldstein family—owners of a restaurant in Putnok—was carrying a toddler and an infant. She was breastfeeding both of them. When we had been traveling for a day, I looked at her face. She was drenched in sweat, drained and dehydrated. Here she was, feeding two babies and trying futilely to keep her breasts covered. It seemed impossible—she certainly couldn't last long.

"Don't look. Look the other way," Mother told me. But she understood the maternal instinct. "If you were that age, I would do the same thing!" she said. "That's what mothers do!"

Again, I tried to imagine where we might be going. I went to the side of the car and the cracks were large enough that I could see out. The train was traveling so fast that it was impossible to focus on the sights as we passed. I saw nothing but cornfields and beautiful green spaces and fields of poppies. Peasants were working, picking fruit. It was agricultural country. I thought about what a beautiful summer day it was—just about the time of year when we used to pick the corn in our garden back home. I closed my mind and pictured the corn and the garden at home and again I cried.

I told Mother what I had seen: just acres and acres of green land and peasants picking corn and fruit.

People said, "That's a good sign!" They wanted so badly for all of this to make sense. They clung to any hope this all might end well. I imagined we were going somewhere where there was life and people were living and harvesting. It was such a hopeful sign to see that we weren't somewhere dark, without human life. Was this where we were going?

Valerie and Viktor—who were just 11 and 7—were crying and shaking. They were frightened. Mother held their hands. We had run out of water and food for them.

I could feel my tongue going dry. We all simply stood and shook and cried.

And prayed.

Mr. Lovy and the other religious Jews put on their *tallises* and they davened. They were shouting and screaming to God: *"Shemisborach!"* —Blessed One—"Why are you allowing this to happen? Where are you?" All I heard was *"Shema Yisroel,"*—Hear O Israel. Just praying and praying and shouting and crying and screaming.

It was so intense and so, so sad. And the stench: People had to go to the bathroom, and the bucket was overflowing. The odor was un-bearable. People were dripping with sweat. If we had towels or hand-kerchiefs we just kept wiping the sweat.

We used whatever we had—scraps of paper, pieces of clothing—to fan ourselves and get some circulation.

People were suffocating from the heat and becoming dehydrated. And then, they began to die. I watched as some of the older men and women's bodies, so weary from the deprivation, began to shut down. Weaker and weaker, they couldn't hold up their heads anymore.

There was one girl from the Schwartz family. Her baby was about six months old, and it just slept. Mother looked at her and gasped: "She can't breath anymore! She can't breathe!" And then, almost whispering: "Her life is over!"

She was not the only one. I watched, in the dim light of the car, the unimaginable horror: one body after another giving out. I was surrounded by corpses. None of us could do anything to help. We tried to hold up people's heads, and they would flop down again. We would close their eyes. *Another corpse, another one, another.* People I had known all my life, but I couldn't help them. And I worried: Who would be next? My brother? My sister? My mother?

Everyone was so sad and stunned.

Jewish tradition prescribes in great detail how one must give dignity to the dead. We wanted to do the right thing. But how could we here? We covered their faces when we could.

The prayer at a funeral is *El maleh rachamim*—God, who is full of mercy. And that just never stopped. *"El maleh rachamim"* over and over. The religious men would ask the survivors, if there were any, the name of the person who had just died. And they would insert it in the prayer, begging God to have mercy on the soul of the deceased.

In my 16 and a half years it was the first time I had seen a dead person. Father had eulogized every Jew who died in Putnok. But he had protected me from anything dark or sad. It was a natural parental instinct, but it left me woefully unprepared for this moment. No one could have been prepared.

I was also unequipped for the emotional changes. I had rarely seen my parents cry. But now Mother was crying. Father had cried when he was taken away. In the cattle car, everyone was crying.

Human dignity had vanished in the face of this inhumane treatment. We were being treated like animals, and many of us lost our human instincts.

It was truly a living nightmare. The train sped and rattled. No one could comprehend what was going on. When you are in such miserable conditions, something happens to your mind. Your mentality changes: You become numb from the pain, from losing so much; you cannot think clearly. You aren't rational anymore. All is obscured and confusing. You feel like an animal. You go like sheep. You don't fight; you don't question. You go along. I couldn't plan or think or be helpful. I stared at the corpses. Mother was crying. My sister and brother were shaking. I tried to hold them, despite my own tears and shaking.

After a day, I was beyond the point of giving privacy to others. I went in my pants. Exhausted, in shock, and numb, I lost the urge to help anyone. I was so miserable.

There aren't enough words in any language to describe the emptiness, the sadness and hopelessness we had.

Now I understood. Father was right: The world was on fire, and we were burning in it.

I was most frightened by the unknown. With all the physical pain, the discomfort and nausea and pain and misery, the hardest part was not knowing what would happen next.

I dealt with my fear through tears and silence. But others prayed. Men stood and davened the traditional prayers, morning noon and night.

Mother said, "This is *Moshiachsayt"* — the time of the Messiah. "After this, what else is left? It couldn't get any worse. We're suffering, we're united: poor and old and young and children, we're all the same. The Messiah must be on the way!"

She knew that Jewish lore said that in the end of days, calamity would precede the ultimate redemption. That's what Father had always told us. She believed — she had to believe — that the Messiah was now imminent. We were near death; most of us were corpses anyway. Mother kept saying, "Just hold on! It's a good thing! It's a good thing! We're all suffering. We're all Jews and we're all here for the same reason. We're all united. There's no difference between young and old, poor and rich: *Moshiach*! "

Over and over, Mother repeated this belief: "Hold on. It's going to be over. Messiah is coming! *Moshiach* is coming!"

And then the train stopped.

It had been two days. It was around 5:00 in the afternoon on Thursday, June 15. A guard opened the door.

5

'You Have the Right to Live'

IMMEDIATELY, I HEARD German guards yelling *"Schnell! Schnell! Schnell!"*—Hurry! Hurry! Hurry!

We stood, one by one, families together, grabbing our backpacks and trying to help each other out.

Where were we?

"This is the end of the line," Mother said. "This must be the place they plan to take us."

The guards ordered us to carry the corpses out of the car. Out of almost 100 people who had entered the car, some 75 left it alive. Some of the dead were infants. We grabbed an arm or a leg or a hand and struggled to drag the bodies until they dropped to the cement beside the tracks. We tried to make sure the faces were covered. The stench was almost unbearable. Mother could not bear to touch the dead; she just held on to Viktor and Valerie.

After the corpses were all out, I looked up.

I saw a sign: AUSCHWITZ.

I had never heard of Auschwitz. I didn't know what it meant. I turned my head to the right and to the left. I looked in front of me and behind me. We were surrounded by electric barbwire. I noticed watchtowers in every corner with SS soldiers carrying heavy machine guns. A searchlight was lit up, even during the day. And I saw German shepherds, growling and barking.

I froze in terror. I saw thousands of men in groups, women in other groups, all wearing striped uniforms with large numbers on the back or front.

What was this place?

Mother got off the cattle car. She grabbed the children's hands and walked around the corpses. There was a fence nearby and on the other side, prisoners. First Mother shouted a prayer, "*Shema Yisroel Adonai Eloheinu Adonai Echad!*" — Hear O Israel, the Lord our God the Lord is One. She was thanking God that we were out of the cattle car. And then she began shouting to the prisoners nearby.

"Mister, do you know Solomon Rosenfeld? We're from Putnok. Have any of you seen my husband?" She was screaming Father's name. "Do you know my son, Yosele Rosenfeld, the cantor? From Budapest?" She kept shouting.

They laughed at her. One prisoner sounded Czech but he spoke Hungarian. He said to his friend, "Look at that crazy woman! She's looking for her husband!" He made a sign twirling an index finger around his head: "*Meshuggeh*" — Crazy. "You know how many husbands are here — and they're nameless!? We have a *number*. We don't have names!"

What did that mean, a number?

"She's crazy," he kept saying. "That's why she ended up here!"

Her voice was hoarse, but she was screaming, searching for Father and Andor. I tried to stop her.

"Stop asking for Dad," I said. "There are too many people here. Just take care of Viktor and Valerie and yourself. Don't waste your voice."

The guards were separating the men from the women, sending men to the right and women to the left. The younger boys stayed with the females. We followed the line of women and they told us to line up in rows of five and walk. We held onto each other's hands. She handed me her little clutch purse with the red marble clip — the one that held her wedding band, the mezuzah, and the house key.

We walked, holding hands. In my right hand I held Valerie's. Valerie held on to Mother, who held on to Viktor, who held on to another woman from Putnok, Mrs. Jordan. We each carried a backpack. Then I noticed one officer—tall, and very handsome. He had white gloves and very shiny boots and a German military uniform covered with medals. He held his gloves in one hand and a silver stick in the other. He was motioning to the right and to the left, to the right and to the left. As we got closer, I realized what he was doing: separating families. I learned later he was Dr. Josef Mengele, the one in charge of the selection.

Our turn came and we passed him by.

"How old are you?" Mengele asked me.

"*Sechzehn*," I said. German for sixteen.

"You go to the left," he said. "*Arbiten! Arbiten! Arbiten!*"—You work.

That left Mother, my sister and brother, and Mrs. Jordan. (Her husband had died about a year earlier.) They all went to the other side, to the right. I took a step or two and saw they weren't following, and I got scared. I did not want to be separated. So I ran toward my mother. I had not run far when a guard saw me. He pointed a gun at me. Mother turned her head and saw me running, and saw the guard pointing his gun at me. A dog was barking angrily.

"Listen to him—go where he tells you," she said. "You have the right to live."

I did. I went back. I kept turning my head back. They were walking. I saw their backs. I watched them walk and walk and walk until their figures faded away and I couldn't see them anymore.

That was the last time I saw my mother, Valerie, or Viktor.

I HAD TO RUN TO CATCH UP to the handful of girls from Putnok still nearby. I started walking with Klari, my friend from Putnok. She was alone. Her father had been sent to a labor camp. On the journey, Klari and two of her older sisters had been taking care of five or six of their younger siblings. The older girls had been sent to the other side with the young children—apparently Mengele had mistaken them for the mothers of the children. That left Klari alone, just as I was.

We walked together. She was half a head taller than I, big-boned with wavy brown hair, and a round face and narrow eyes and a turned-up nose. Klari was an outgoing, friendly girl. As soon as we knew we were out of earshot of the guards, we made a pact.

"Klari," I said. "Neither of us have anyone. We're both alone. We have to stay together. You're going to be my family. I'm going to be yours."

Klari agreed.

We all kept walking. A guard finally said, "Stop." We were still outside. The sun was starting to go down. Bright lights and searchlights blazed all around.

We stopped. Shouting into megaphones, the guards told us to drop our backpacks. Mine was the navy blue pack with leather straps I had packed in the last days in our home and then carried all the way from Putnok. It had Father's war medals, his *siddur*, the candlesticks and kiddush cup—things I knew we could never replace. It had the things I needed to care for myself: soap, toothpaste, a towel, a washcloth, underwear, stockings, a dress, a sweater and a sheet. It had one more precious item, our family album: a thick, green-covered album with photographs going back to my parents' childhoods, photos of their parents and siblings, our cousins.

It seemed to contain my whole life—or what was left of it.

"Drop it," the guard ordered.

I let the straps slide off my shoulder, and the pack slid to the ground.

There was no time to mourn the loss. Guards were shouting at us to undress. I felt so embarrassed—in front of other women, and the male guards. *"Schnell, Schnell, Schnell!"* they said. "Undress!" I dropped my clothes right there—the pink skirt my sister had given me, the pink blouse.

I thought of my earrings—the ones with three turquoise stones that had saved my life when I was so ill at two and a half. If the guards saw them they would surely take them. So I took them off and hid them in Mother's clutch purse. There had been no time to put it in my backpack, so I was holding it.

A male guard shaved my hair—the hair on my head as well as all of my body hair. I tried to hide the purse under my arm and hold it tightly to my body. While they shaved under one of my arms, I put it under the other.

Then they started to spray me with some kind of disinfectant. (We surely smelled from all the sweat.) I had to raise my arms; I put the purse between my legs and held it tight. I just wanted to save it. But I was standing there naked. And I had to walk. The guards were watching. So as I walked, the clutch purse fell on the soil of Auschwitz. And I cried because of my earrings—the ones that had saved my life, the earrings that had been my good-luck charm.

The guards gave me a prison gown—a long, gray gown of heavy linen. They gave me a pair of Dutch wooden slippers that were much too large for me.

Then a man held out a long, rusty needle.

"Put up your arm," he ordered.

I held out my left arm. I didn't know why. He used the filthy needle to write a number on my forearm.

I looked at it: A17923.

I couldn't imagine what the number was or why they were doing this. In my naïveté I thought, perhaps it was a good thing that they were giving me a number. After all, I must have been an important person to have a special number. I didn't think they were doing it to break our spirits even more than they already had. It bled a little bit, but I didn't have anything to wipe it—not a handkerchief, not underwear.

I didn't know at the time the number would be permanent. I had seen tattoos from the World War. But not on Jews—on gentiles. They would have their name or different symbols. Jews didn't get tattoos. It was against Jewish law. I didn't know what to think. I had never seen a human being with a number until I got mine. Then Klari was after me. The numbers got higher with each person. Klari's was one larger than mine.

The whole operation was efficient, organized and systematic. On both sides of the line I saw piles of backpacks and clothing. Prisoners came and picked up everything—our clothes and backpacks.

The guards ordered us—300 young women—into a small room. Everybody tried to stretch out on the concrete floor. It was so crowded that each of us had our head in someone's lap. What could we do? We prayed and cried. We still hadn't been given any water or food. Nobody told us anything. I yearned for my mother, for my siblings. I wanted to be home—in my father's lap, around the Shabbat table, eating, talking, and singing. But there were no mothers here. No siblings. No home.

A few people from Putnok were around me. We were just shaking and crying. Klari's head was in my lap. As I tried to sleep, I wondered what had become of Mother, Valerie, and Viktor.

6

Auschwitz

I AWOKE TO THE PIERCING SOUNDS of a whistle blowing. It was still dark. "Get up! Get up!" the guards were shouting.

We all went outside. A bright half-moon lit up the sky. The guards shouted to line up in rows of five. They started counting us: *one, two, three, four, five*. We stood there outside for two hours.

It must have been around 4 a.m. The sun was starting to light the horizon and the guards brought large, heavy, metal containers of black coffee. Each row of five got an aluminum bowl of coffee. We each took a few sips, making sure the girls around us would also get sips. They gave us each a slice of yellowish, heavy bread. It was so dense and in my mouth it tasted like sawdust. I had perfect teeth, no cavities. But I couldn't bite into it. I told the girls to leave a little coffee so we could dip the bread in it. We all dipped it in so we were able to bite and chew the bread.

That was our first breakfast in Auschwitz.

The guards ordered us into a larger barrack — about 1,000 girls into each long, dark, dimly lit room. I was in Block 10, C Lager. In the middle was an open walkway; on the sides were wooden bunk beds, three levels to each bunk. I wondered where the mattresses and pillows and covers were; the beds were just wood. They ordered four of us to take each level—12 girls to a bunk bed.

I didn't want to climb too high to get to bed and I didn't want to be stuck in the middle.

"Let's take the bottom," I told Klari. "That way if anything happens, we'll be the first ones out." We chose a bed not too far from the door. Four of us shared it—Klari and I and two others from Putnok: Martha Koth, who was my age, and her sister Lenke, who was two years older.

We stretched out. I felt so tired I could have slept on a rock. We all fell asleep.

Around noon, the guards woke us again and brought heavy containers—this time with soup. They gave everyone a bowl. The soup had all kinds of vegetables: potatoes, turnips, carrots. It was very thick soup, but almost tasteless.

We spent that afternoon on the bed, talking, praying, wondering what would happen next. When I had to find a lavatory, I discovered the only option was an open latrine outside. There was a washroom attached to the barrack. It had water dripping from narrow, rusty pipes. No soap. No towels. The water was so rusty you couldn't drink it. Later, I would catch a drop or two to rinse my mouth or wash out my eyes in the morning. (That toxic, horrible water would ruin my gums and teeth.)

In the evening the guards brought cold cuts—canned, processed meat, like Spam in round slices. I kept kosher, so I looked at it and thought *chazzer*—pig. I would not eat it. Nor would the Koth girls; they were Orthodox, too. There was marmalade and margarine, so we ate that. Klari ate the meat—she was not as religious.

That night I tried to sleep on the bunk. I said my evening prayers. And I talked with the other girls until we started fading off to sleep. We still had on our prison gowns. There were no clothes to change into. We held on to each other; that's all we had—each other's body heat. We were each other's covers.

FOR TWO DAYS WE REPEATED that relentless routine: lining up in fives, being counted, sitting on the bunk beds, eating the sawdust bread and drinking dabs of the bland soup. We followed the orders of a woman named Elsa, a stunning, dark-haired Jewish girl from Czechoslovakia. She was the *Blockalteste*, the commander for our block. She alternated shifts with Felicia, who had beautiful skin—like marble—and a third girl, Rachel, a red-haired beauty from Czechoslovakia. They were all gorgeous. I learned later that the Nazis would take the most beautiful and shapely Jewish girls, put them in charge of the block as the *kapos,* and use them as their mistresses. The *Blockaltestes* wore regular, nice civilian clothes and stockings and their hair was shiny and clean.

In exchange, these women turned into cruel, brutal monsters, shouting and screaming and beating prisoners for no reason at all. It was work the German officers didn't want to do; they wanted to stay away from the prisoners. The kapos each had a stick and a leather belt. They were mean and harsh and horrible, slapping women left and right. They made sure there was no panic and that everyone behaved. It was their job, what they did to keep themselves alive. It was a cruel irony of the place that the most beautiful women were doing some of the ugliest work.

The second day we were finished with the morning headcount when I looked across the tall barbwire fence and saw a familiar face—a young rabbi named Avrohum who had married a girl from Putnok. I called to him, and when he realized I was from Putnok he started asking me about his family. Of course, I knew nothing. With guards watching, he couldn't talk, so he began writing on something and threw it over the fence to me. It was a lemon. He had carved a message on it: He had been deported from his Czechoslovakian town long ago, and had no idea of anyone's fate. Then he wrote five more words.

"Auschwitz is hell, hell, hell."

AFTER A COUPLE OF DAYS, Elsa sent us to work, assigning us seemingly at random. I was dispatched to the kitchen, where my job was peeling and cutting up vegetables. I did that for two weeks, just cutting turnips and carrots and potatoes.

It was difficult to be around so much food when I felt so hungry and we were so cruelly undernourished. One day, I spotted loaves of bread on a rack. I looked around to see if anyone was looking. There was one guard, but I waited until he turned his back. I grabbed a loaf. My heart raced. I slipped the loaf into the hem of my prison gown. (I was so short that the gown reached the ground.) I held onto the hem as I walked back to the barrack.

I knew that by smuggling food like that I was putting my life at risk. If I had been caught, I risked severe punishment. They could have denied me food, at best. I had seen prisoners beaten for lesser offenses. But every day, I would try to sneak bread or vegetables or anything else I could to share with the other girls. I never came back empty handed.

Despite my fear of getting caught, I knew that I was doing a *mitzvah*—the mitzvah of saving lives. I knew that if you were doing a mitzvah—following God's commandments—you were supposed to be rewarded. Each time I would say a prayer. I never got caught.

The counting repeated every day. One guard would make sure there were five in each row; another counted the rows. They had to have an exact count every morning.

One day during the counting, one of the guards told us that if we did extra chores, we could get extra food. I felt so hungry and I wanted to stay as healthy as I could. So I waited to hear what the job would be.

"We need girls to give manicures and pedicures to the officers," she said. I had always been the one at home to cut my younger brother's and sister's fingernails and toenails. So I knew I could do that. I raised my hand.

The next morning, after the counting and coffee and bread, I reported for duty. The officers sat on big, comfortable chairs just outside the barrack. A kapo gave me scissors and a nail file. The first officer held out his hand. There were no words. I began clipping with the scissors, then filing. We didn't talk. The officer looked at it. *"Shun, shun!"* he said—"Nice." I did that for an hour, and each time earned a small extra loaf of bread.

One day in the morning lineup they told us they had another job.

"Who can do shaves for the officers?" she asked.

The Germans were almost all clean-shaven, but they were also lazy. Why should they shave themselves? With this whole camp full of slave labor, why not use it?

I immediately volunteered. I wanted to seem eager and willing, a good worker. There was only one major problem. I had never seen a razor blade in my life! Father always had a long beard, and my older brothers had beards. Even when they trimmed their beards, Orthodox men didn't shave with metal blades. In their strict reading of Jewish law, that was forbidden. They had wooden shavers and soap to help soften the whiskers.

The first morning they assigned me to shave a high-ranking officer, a rotund, middle-aged man wearing shiny boots and a chest bedecked with all kinds of medals. He took off his jacket and took a towel. I took a blade in my hand and examined the sharp blade and the soap and the brush. *What if I cut him?* I thought. I worried that my hands would shake, just from nerves. I said a prayer: "*Shema Yisroel,* God of Israel, I need the bread. I'm good with my hands. You gave me talent. Let me use it."

I always believed there was a higher power accompanying me. And I had the will to live.

I lathered his face and began to shave, trying carefully to judge what kind of pressure would cut the hairs but not his skin. It was all so unfamiliar. Miraculously, my hands stayed steady. I finished the shave. He stood up and left.

I didn't have time to breathe a sigh. The next officer sat down. A new challenge: He had a mustache. That seemed to be an art form in itself, working around a mustache. What to cut? What to leave? How short to trim it? It wasn't easy. But again, I survived. No blood. No scratches. I believed that God must have wanted me to have that extra bread so I could keep going.

The pattern continued: the counting, the minimal food. Whenever they would ask for volunteers, I raised my hand—for the bread, to look eager. If what they needed was workers, I would be their best worker. I wanted to live.

Yet it didn't take long to understand that Auschwitz was a place

My family in October, 1937. Left to right: my sister Aranka; me (at age 10);
my mother Rozsi holding baby Viktor; my sister Valerie and brother
Andor (standing); my father Solomon; my brother Sandor; and my sister Irene.

The synagogue
in Putnok,
destroyed in
the war. I took
this photo of
the ruins
on a visit
in 1971.

At right: My mother Rozsi and her
brother Moishe during the
First World War. Moishe wears
a Hungarian army uniform.

Below: My mother at age 37.

Bottom left, My grandfather,
Abraham Rosenfeld, photographed
in the early 1920s.

My brother Andor, a cantor in
Budapest in a photo from 1942,
before he went to a forced labor
camp in Koszeg, Hungary. There he
became sick with tetanus and later
froze to death.

Above:
Auschwitz,
main entrance.

At right:
an Auschwitz
guard tower
and electrified
barbed wire.

My husband Ernie (second
from the left) at a slave
labor camp in Sarospatak,
Hungary in 1942.

I'm on the far right,
posing just after liberation
in the dress I sewed
from a blue and white
mattress cover.

My brother Sandor,
who died in 1948,
fighting for
Israel's independence.

My sisters,
photographed
in 1943.
Each would survive
Bergen-Belsen:
Irene at right, and
Aranka at far right.

My husband
Ernie in
1947.

This portrait of me is also from 1947.

Uncle Sheeya, B'nai B'rak Israel, 1967.

I'm seated in the center at a family wedding. Ernie is behind me in white;
next to me are my sisters Irene (far left) and (next to her) Aranka.

In the decade I have been a public speaker, I have met many wonderful people, including Holocaust historian Deborah Lipstadt (above, left); and director Steven Spielberg (above, right).

I love telling my story to children in their classrooms or on their visits to the Museum of Tolerance in Los Angeles. I always bring my camera to take a picture of the audience.

My family in 2006. From left: Nancy, Kimberly, me, Sandy and her husband Steve.

consumed with death.

Everywhere I looked, guards patrolled with machine guns. If they were in the mood, they would use them, often with no warning. The slightest offense—or no offense at all—could set off a guard. Every day I saw a guard beating somebody, or shooting someone to death. I never felt safe.

Every detail of Auschwitz seemed designed to impart fear: Vicious dogs trained to attack prisoners; searchlights everywhere. And the whole camp was surrounded by electrified barbwire. All too often, those who just could not take it anymore touched the wire, ending their lives in an instant. Many people did that. Klari and I watched them walking closer and closer to the wire, their faces pained with lost hope. We screamed to stop them.

"Don't do it! Have hope!" we called. "Give yourself a chance." But we could never stop them. The suffering had consumed them. They touched the wire and died immediately from the electrical shock.

The most terrifying thing was the unknown. From one instant to the next, I never knew who would be the next one to be shot or beaten or tortured. At any moment, none of us knew what the next moment would bring. This made Auschwitz a hell on earth. There was no peace.

Still, I never considered trying to escape. I never wanted to. And it would have been impossible. Guards watched from high watchtowers with searchlights. They tracked our every movement. When people tried to escape they were shot. I would just wait it out, be patient, and follow orders. I wouldn't do anything to risk my life.

But I escaped every day in my mind. While I worked, I fantasized; I let my imagination wander and I planned my future. I thought about how I was going to have a boyfriend. I planned my wedding. I imagined my children and how I wanted to raise them. I considered how I would rebuild my life. I had always wanted to be a wife and a mother, so I occupied my mind dreaming about what was still to come. I pondered how in some miraculous way I would make it home to Putnok and find my family. (Not everyone could do that; Klari, for one, was a much more concrete thinker. She knew she was in Auschwitz, and that's what she thought about: Auschwitz.)

Sometimes the dreams were just that: dreams. One night I dreamt that I was in our kitchen in Putnok. We had just finished a big family meal, and I was helping Mother.

"Leah," Mother said in the dream. "Will you help me dry the dishes?" The maid had been helping her but she had to leave.

I reached for a towel.

"Uh, uh, uh! Not this one!" she scolded me. "This is for *milchig.*" Of course, we had a kosher kitchen with two sets of dishes: one for dairy, one for meals with meat. We had separate towels, too. "The other is for meat," she told me.

I woke up and found myself tangled with the other girls in the bunk bed. It had seemed so real, and I felt so sad to find myself back in the grim reality of Auschwitz. I wished I could have made the dream last longer.

All of my nighttime dreams were about home, school and Putnok. I never dreamt about the guards watching us. I believed my dreams were God's way of helping me through those frightening nights.

By day, it was harder to keep going amid the deprivation, death and despair. But three things helped me to carry on: friendship, attitude and faith.

Most people were truly alone in Auschwitz. That was by design. The Germans had separated us from our loved ones, robbing us of the men in our families, and then brutally tearing mothers and children apart at the gates of Auschwitz. So most people lived in isolation, merely looking out for themselves. But God blessed me in that dark place with a companion: Klari.

Klari and I looked out for each other. She was always right next to me. It wasn't easy, but we worked very hard to avoid being separated. Whenever the guards ordered us into groups of five, we would be sure to line up in the same group.

We weren't alike in all ways; I was more religious and Klari would even tease me that I prayed too much. But it made a huge difference having someone to care for.

It gave me one more reason to keep going.

"Smile! Stand up straight!" I would tell her. "Show that you are strong!"

When I reminded her, I reminded myself of what I had observed: If we could give the appearance of strength and vitality, we had a much greater chance of survival. The Nazis hated when people looked down and out. They wanted cheerful people who were able to work. I saw that when prisoners looked weak—pale, hunched over, sad—they quickly became targets. The Nazis would just take them out and shoot them.

So I did everything possible to look healthy. I was short, but I stood on my tiptoes. I tried to have good posture. I pinched my cheeks so they would look nice and rosy. If I noticed we were looking pale again—we were so undernourished and scared—I would take a pocketknife or a fork and prick my finger to get a drop of blood, and then smear it on my cheeks to make them look healthier.

And I always smiled. I knew if you were angry and bitter they had no use for you. If you smiled and showed that you were willing to follow orders, they trusted you. I smiled.

And then there was my faith. I woke up each morning hoping for a better day. I tried to keep my spirits high. No matter how bad it got, I kept my spirit up and my prayers with me. I always had faith that God was with me and that I was going to go home. I never believed anyone would hurt me. I was determined to fight for my life.

I didn't care if they deprived me of food; my system got used to it. After a while, your body adjusts and your stomach doesn't growl anymore. If the kapo hit me with a leather belt, I just thought I could take anything. But I was not going to let them take my soul away. I knew that if I had my *neshama*—my soul—and my emotions and my memory then I was still a human being, no matter how hungry or thin, no matter how much pain I felt.

I wanted to be a witness, to tell the world what happened to the Jewish people. So I knew I would never give up. I would never touch the electric wire. I would fight for my life every day.

Even with that faith, I had moments when I feared the worst. It was hard to escape death. One morning during daily counting, a guard ordered Klari and me to go pile onto a flatbed truck with canvas sides. I had seen these trucks driving around the camp with prisoners standing or sitting on the back. They would load onto it and then it would suddenly take off. I thought they were being taken to work somewhere. But that morning, after we were ordered onto it, I heard some horrifying words from another prisoner nearby.

"The people who get on that truck aren't going to work," a prisoner said. "They're taken and murdered."

I realized that he must have been right. I had seen the truck leave with people many times. But it always came back empty.

We had no choice. As the menacing armed guards stood by, Klari and I climbed onto the truck, along with about one hundred people.

"Everyone lie down!" the guard ordered.

We lay down on our stomachs. And with this mass of people lying horizontally, they stretched a canvas over us, secured it tightly and tied it down. Klari and I held hands, frightened. The driver sped for about 15 minutes, then suddenly stopped.

A huge gust of wind had kicked up, blowing so much dust and debris that the driver couldn't see and couldn't proceed. Tumbleweeds were blowing all around.

"Open it up!" I yelled to Klari.

She loosened the rope, so there was a small opening in the canvas.

"Jump!" I said.

"*You* jump!" She replied.

We leapt from the truck and slipped behind some tumbleweed. Klari was shaking. She could barely breathe. We lay there, hiding and holding hands.

"I'm so scared," she said.

"I'm scared, too," I replied.

We stood there behind the huge tumbleweed. We held our breath and waited, terrified that we'd be found out. It seemed like an eternity. But after a couple of minutes, the driver sped off. I felt so tired. I had hardly any life left in me. But we got up. It was a miracle. The wind had given us a break, and then I had the good sense to open the canvas and run. Klari and I waited there for hours, trying to stay out of sight. When it was close to sunset, we saw a group of prisoners marching back toward the barracks. We joined them.

We never saw the people who had been taken on the truck that day. As far we knew, they had all been taken out and shot.

TWO WEEKS AFTER MY ARRIVAL I experienced my first selection. The guards were ordering groups of girls in different directions. I did my best to stay with the same group: Klari and the Koth sisters. They ordered probably 300 of us in one direction and took us toward the train tracks. There, they forced us back into the very kind of cattle cars we had come in. We had no idea where we were going. They simply said we were headed to a place where our work was needed. Nobody gave us a clue where.

Again, the door slammed shut and the car began rolling. It was the first time I had left Auschwitz since arriving with Mother and my brother and sister. Now I wondered if I was leaving them there. How would I ever find them? How long would this journey be? A few minutes? Hours? Days?

It had been less than three hours when the train slowed to a halt. The doors opened, suddenly. I saw signs that said PLASZOW and KRAKOW.

"Where are we?" I asked people. Someone said it was another camp. I saw more barracks, more barbwire.

They put us to work at the Krakow Jewish cemetery. It was humiliating and depressing work: using sledgehammers to destroy tombstones. We worked from sunrise to sunset, only stopping for breakfast, lunch and dinner. Krakow had a large Jewish population and the cemetery was full of the tombs of great rabbis and scholars—the best in the world. Each one had Hebrew letters spelling out the names—Yitzhak, Yaakov, Hershel—and a *Magen David*, a Jewish star, or some other Jewish symbol.

This was truly sinister. The Germans hated the Jews so much they wouldn't even let Jewish corpses rest in peace. They wanted to destroy every Jew—living or dead—one way or another. And they used

Jews to do it. As I broke the precious memorial stones, I felt something in me break, too. But we had to follow orders, busting one stone into 10 pieces. Another prisoner then pushed over a cart and hauled away the broken pieces. Like the others, I had very little strength; I was malnourished and weak. Sometimes it took five or six of us to break a single stone.

In Plaszow's barracks, where I shared a bed with Klari and the other girls, we had blankets—a step up from Auschwitz, but not much: still no mattress or pillow. They fed us slightly more, but the food was still bland and tasteless.

We encountered a different breed of guards. Most of them were Polish political prisoners—people accused of being communists. And they could be brutal. One was a huge peasant named Josef, who walked around brandishing a leather belt. He would lash the prisoners for no reason at all. One afternoon, noticing my slackening pace, he struck me in the shoulder, wounding me so badly that years later the injury showed up in an x-ray.

In Plaszow, I met watchmakers and jewelers with experience working with rings and necklaces. One area of the camp had a garage-like structure where these men had set up shop, serving the German officers, who loved jewelry. Some of the Germans had a watch on each arm and rings on every finger. Seeing it, I imagined the people from whom they'd stolen it all—imagined Jews from Hungary and Germany and Poland arriving at Auschwitz to have their valuables stripped from their bodies, just as I had lost my earrings and Mother's engagement ring.

After the backbreaking labor in the cemetery, they put us to work on another brutal task: using picks and sledgehammers in an attempt to flatten the top of a mountain (the same mountain I saw later in the film *Schindler's List*). Meanwhile, the men were building more barracks for the huge influxes of prisoners.

Just as in Auschwitz, I watched people become weaker and weaker and fade away. I knew one pair of sisters. One got weaker and weaker —from hunger, from being beaten, from typhus that had begun to spread. Finally, she died, and the other had to close the dead girl's eyes. I promised myself that would not happen to me. I never thought my time would come; I simply willed myself to live. I didn't want to bury myself alive. I knew God was with me. I stayed hopeful.

Those hopes were buoyed when we got word we would be leaving this miserable and degrading place. In early September, five weeks after we had arrived, they loaded us back in a cattle car. Again, nobody told us where we were going. There was no communication. The doors shut, and we rode for another two hours.

WHEN THE TRAIN STOPPED, they opened the doors. It looked familiar. I recognized the gates: We were back at Auschwitz. It felt like a crushing blow. *My God,* I thought. *We were here once. Why are they bringing us back?*

7

'Do You Know What That Smoke Is?'

THIS TIME, I WOULD LEARN the gruesome truth about what Auschwitz was all about.

I was able to stay with Klari and the girls again. We were in a different barrack, No. 9, but the routine was more or less the same.

They sent me to work in the laundry, delivering disinfected blankets to a warehouse in Birkenau, one of the subcamps in Auschwitz. As incentive, the guards promised us that when we got there, we could visit our relatives or get a chance to write them postcards.

That was enough for me. I had wondered every day what had become of my family. Not just about my mother and the two younger children: I wondered about Aranka and Irene in Budapest. And about Andor and Sandor, who had been forced into labor camps. I didn't know anything. Were they alive? Were they free? Would I ever see them? No one in Auschwitz could tell me.

So the promise of making contact was all the motivation I needed.

Instead, I got a horrifying education. One day, when I arrived from the laundry to deliver disinfected blankets, I met the Zondercommandos—Jews, Pols and Greeks whose job was to work in Birkenau. They told me some of them had been there three or four years. One man got my attention when he spoke to me in Yiddish.

"Do you know what they're doing here?" he asked. He pointed toward the towering chimney, at the smoke billowing out.

"Do you know what that smoke is?" he asked.

I shook my head.

He told me what had happened when we arrived: The guards had taken our loved ones, telling them they were going to take a shower. They were ordered to go to the bathhouse to take a shower.

The guards told them to undress, he said, and to put everything in one pile. The mothers tied the children's little shoes together, to make sure that after the showers, they would be able to find the matching pairs. They were so meticulous—the mothers had placed their clothes together with their children's. Then they all marched in and waited for the shower.

"When they turn on the faucet, " he said. "Instead of water, there is gas—deadly gas."

I stood there listening, unable to speak.

"Then they are all cremated—young, old, infants, everyone—in a few minutes. Their lives are over," he said "We are the ones who carry the corpses to be incinerated."

I looked at him, stunned.

"How long have you been here?" I asked.

"Since 1939," he said. The others with him said 1940 or '41.

They've been here so long, I thought, they've all gone crazy.

"Are you *meshuggeh?*" I asked.

"We're telling you the truth," said one.

"*Toras Emes! Toras Emes!*" said another man. The true Torah. "It's *takeh, takeh!*" It's the truth.

I did not believe them.

I knew it could not be true.

Still, I felt ill. I had seen so much cruelty already, I feared what they said might have a grain of truth. And I kept witnessing the smoke spewing from the chimney. I would see corpses on wheelbarrows. One moment I tried to dismiss it, but the next I figured it must be true, since so many of them were describing the same things.

"Get out of Auschwitz," one of the men said. "Get yourself in a selection and get out of here. Auschwitz is a killing factory."

8

Anything to Survive

I F I DIDN'T BELIEVE IT THEN, I came to believe it soon enough. They assigned me to some of the most heartbreaking work imaginable: sorting the belongings that had been confiscated from prisoners upon their arrival. Just as I had, millions of inmates had been forced to drop their belongings within minutes of their arrival. My new job was to go through those items, opening backpacks and taking out whatever we found: children's clothing, tiny toddlers' shoes, dolls. We put them in piles according to category and size.

For a while, I gathered the piles of hair that guards had shaven off the new arrivals and put it in piles. I saw the wigs that countless Orthodox women had worn and been forced to discard. That hurt was intensified as I remembered Mother's wig; I thought it must be somewhere amid these piles.

It was emotional and painful work. The guards had removed teeth from many of the prisoners and we had to put those in piles. Everything had its own pile: eyeglasses, coats, prayer books, children's shoes. There were *tzitzis*—the garments with fringes worn by Orthodox boys and men—and *tallises*—prayer shawls. I saw disassembled Torah scrolls. Allowed just one piece of luggage, people had actually carried their communities' precious Torahs from their homes to this godforsaken place. And the Germans forced us to dissect them.

Sorting it all out was a huge job, requiring the labor of thousands of men and women. We separated not just the contents, but also the suitcases themselves, arranging them by country of origin. I saw names and addresses on suitcases, or sometimes just the country: Poland, Hungary, Czechoslovakia. And I wondered about the person who had carried each one. Who had they been? A rabbi? A tailor? A farmer? Somebody's boyfriend? Somebody's little girl?

The worst assignment was extracting gold teeth from corpses of people who had been beaten or starved to death. The guard would give me a knife and a chisel and we had to remove the gold from the mouth and put it in a pile. One of us would hold the head while another would extract the gold. We did that over and over again, tossing the gold into a large sack. It was awful, gruesome work. I would wonder: Whose brother is this? Whose son is this? They had taken such good care of their teeth and now look what was happening.

But I had to do it, because I knew that if I didn't, I could well be next.

I became numb. Immune. I lost all feeling. I was just doing a job, like a doctor performing surgery without thinking about the patient. The pain of focusing was too great—and if you paused to moan or cry, the guards would beat you. So I just did the job. It was simply a matter of survival.

One day Klari and I had to sort the children's shoes. It broke my heart. Here were all these shoes. But where were the children? Finally, the truth began to sink in. I looked at one tiny pair of shoes and realized they would have fit my brother Viktor. Maybe they were his shoes.

Maybe those men had been telling me the truth about the showers.

And I began to wonder again whom I would find when I got home. I realized that even if I was able to survive, there might be no one left. I had to put that in the back of my mind. I had to live. I had to take care of myself. I had to make each and every day a day of survival.

I LEARNED TO TAKE ANY opportunity to get a bit of extra food for my friends and myself. Sometimes that meant taking risks.

Often, when we were outside being counted, I would hear music. At first I thought it was a radio somewhere. But it kept getting closer and closer. One day I was in the barrack when I looked outside and saw a group of musicians with all kinds of instruments. The Germans loved classical music; they would come from wherever they were to hear it. The guards would stand and smoke cigarettes or cigars or pipes and listen to the music.

I saw a wooden stand with extra instruments on it. The guards were shouting, asking if anyone knew how to play the instruments.

"Are any of you musicians?" they asked.

I looked up and all of these musicians seemed very professional. I looked at a violin and remembered how Father would take out his violin on Purim and play Yiddish songs. As a child, I had studied about the classical composers and I had gone to the opera a few times a year. But I had never played, and the violin looked too complicated. Then I noticed a flute. I thought that looked simple; I could pretend to play the flute.

I raised my hand.

"Go, go!" the guards urged me. *"Arous! Arous!"*

I picked up a flute. There were three or four rows of musicians. I elbowed my way to the back row, in the middle. I thought if I stayed there, nobody would watch me closely enough to notice that I was only pretending to play.

They started playing the song "Blue Danube." I raised the flute to my mouth and moved my fingers. I didn't even blow. The musicians on either side of me—most of them were from Germany and Austria—gave me looks, as if to say: "What are you doing here?"

I just tried to concentrate.

"Bitte, bitte, bitte!" I said. "Please don't say anything." My stomach was tied in a knot. They looked at each other and took pity. Nobody said a word. I couldn't wait for it to end.

Luckily, the guards were just happy. Many of them seemed drunk. They frequently drank too much beer. They were in a cheerful mood.

There was loud applause; they were jubilant, and we put down the instruments on the stand.

For that I received an extra loaf of bread. I ran inside and found Klari.

"Eva," she said. "I didn't know you played an instrument!"

I smiled. "Keep your mouth shut," I said. "Today I did."

Everyone pulled the bread apart, enjoying the small feast.

I did that twice. I was terrified—but it was worth it. Not only did I eat, but I shared with many others who desperately needed the bread. I asked some of the other girls to join me but they didn't want to pretend. They were afraid of being caught—and shot. They feared that if the guards caught on, they might collectively punish the entire block, randomly selecting dozens of people for death.

It was a big risk I took for the others and myself. I always said a prayer: *Shema Yisroel*. But I just felt safe, thinking God would help me, that God wanted me to get that extra food and share it with the others. When you want to share food to save your life and save others, your fear disappears.

Afterwards, I thought giving manicures and shaving was easier. Pretending to play the flute was shaky.

KLARI HELPED KEEP ME alive in many ways. One day as we were being counted, the guards were walking around with trained German shepherds. They wanted to have a little fun, so they let the dogs loose. One of them attacked me, charging at me and taking a chunk out of my right leg. I was in excruciating pain. The blood was flowing through my prison gown and all around. I was crying and screaming with pain. The guard pulled the dog away. I stood there with a puddle of blood, in wrenching pain, Klari at my side.

Besides the pain, I felt fear. If the bleeding didn't stop, the Germans would surely let me bleed to death. I cried even more.

I couldn't walk—or even hop. Somehow Klari helped get me into the barrack. I went inside. Near the doorway, I saw a piece of raggedy, dark-blown blanket. It was full of lice and dust. Someone had left it there. I picked it up. I told Klari to hold one end and pull it as tight as she could around my leg, creating a tourniquet. We wrapped it as tightly as we could around my leg. The blood was still bubbling through, soaking the blanket. Eventually it stopped. I lay down on the wooden bed in awful pain, but finally I fell asleep.

The next morning, in the bathhouse area, I held my leg up and Klari held it near the faucet where the rusty water was dripping. I saw the huge gash. It was a miracle that it wasn't bleeding anymore. After that I went two or three times a day when I could and tried to wash it. There were no towels to wipe it with. I was limping. But I thought if the guards saw me limping, they would kill me. Klari was always behind me, holding my shoulder as we walked from place to place to make sure I wasn't limping. She covered for me.

Without her I would have just stayed there where the dog had bitten me and been killed. Others would have thought, *I don't want to deal with that; it's her leg. I don't want to get involved.* They had their own problems. They didn't know whether the dog might jump at them next. As much as people wanted to help, they rarely did, because so much was at stake. While you were helping the injured person, you could be hurting yourself. It wasn't easy to be a friend in Auschwitz. But Klari and I had made a pact together. And we honored it. That was my security blanket. We were there for each other.

At times that meant we did things that neither of us might have had the stomach to do alone. In my last days in Auschwitz, I was ill, and getting weaker with each passing day. They had told us the Germans feared that the enemy was getting close, so they were considering liquidating the camp and they were going to kill as many of us as they could.

Frail and unable to work, I was determined to hide. I looked next door in Block 11 and saw a lot of lice-ridden canvas blankets draped over people apparently lying around on the ground. I lifted the corner of one blanket and was shocked with the sight: a dead body. I recalled that Block 11 was where they deposited the bodies of people who died from beatings or from touching the electrified wires. Everyone knew. We could often smell the awful stench of human flesh.

I was growing weak and needed a place where I wouldn't be spotted and taken away. So I told Klari to follow me that night after they turned out the lights in the barrack. That night, she followed me into Block 11. We grabbed a blanket from a couple of the corpses and covered ourselves. The smell was horrible. We held our noses.

The guards would walk around and sometimes they would get close to us and even kick us in the shin to see if we would move—just to have fun. We held our breath until the guards passed. Then we started breathing again and went in search of a scrap of potato or piece of bread. This went on for a couple of days; we hid by day and snuck back to the barrack at night. We had no choice. This was for survival. We would do anything to ward off death.

Somehow, we kept track of the calendar. One afternoon I heard a man shout from the other side of a high fence "Tomorrow is Yom Kippur!" Yom Kippur is the holiest day of the Jewish year, ordinarily a solemn day of prayer and fasting. In Auschwitz we did our best to honor that. We didn't eat. I drank, because it was so hot. I didn't want to take the chance of becoming dehydrated and passing out. With the other girls, I said my prayers using a prayer book I had acquired from another prisoner in a secret exchange for food. We took turns, because we each wanted to stand when we said the *Amida*, the standing, private prayer that is the center of every Jewish service. Two or three of us stood outside and prayed and kept an eye out for the guards.

I relived the past over and over again in my mind, imagining my home life in Putnok. I recalled the holidays of previous years—when I had been with my family, at home and in shul. Even ordinary days were difficult, but holidays were intensely sad.

When we had selections, prisoners tried to get selected to go anywhere—because no one survived in Auschwitz. Anything was better. We had been back in Auschwitz for about three weeks when one day in September, just after Yom Kippur, at one selection they said they needed 500 girls as workers somewhere. (They never said where.) We all went together: Klari and I and the Koth girls. Remarkably, the four of us were able to stay together.

Once again, they piled us into cattle cars. We traveled at least two hours or so before the train pulled to a halt.

9

Respite at Last

WHEN THE DOORS OPENED and we started climbing out of the cattle car, I could see a large warehouse in what looked like an industrial area. The signs said AUGSBURG.

Before long, we learned that this was not a camp; it was a factory in German territory where they fabricated airplane parts.

Right away, it felt like a different world from Auschwitz. The SS guards turned us over to guards from the Wehrmacht, the general ranks of the German military, and the difference was immediately striking. Right away, they let us take showers. It was the first time I had been able to wash my body in months—since we were home in Putnok—and the water felt luxurious as it fell on my body.

They took our prison gowns and the wooden slippers and gave us fresh clothes: blue and white factory uniforms, regular lace-up shoes, underwear, slips and kerchiefs. They showed us the sleeping quarters: regular twin-size beds with blankets and pillows. Klari and I looked at each other in awe. Each of us was going to have her own space.

God is with us, I thought. *God helped us get away from the SS.*

Right away, they put us to work on the assembly line making airplane parts.

The Germans needed to manufacture more and better planes to stand up to the air power of the Allies. And they didn't treat us like prisoners. They treated us as factory workers should be treated.

The people who trained us were French political prisoners. They taught me to run a machine called the Dreyaraier, making parts for the airplane wings. I made tiny screws and the next person on the line would screw the part on the wing. The foreman had to set up and put the screw in the machine. In order to fit it on the wing, you had to take parts of it off. Then somebody else came and measured it before we put it onto the wing.

It wasn't difficult work. I learned quickly, and I was very productive.

Compared to everything else we had lived through, this was heaven. The people in charge were much more humane and compassionate than any I had encountered in many months. We were treated like human beings. No longer did we have to endure the endless sessions of head counts that had punctuated our lives in Auschwitz. I didn't see anyone being beaten or harmed. Nobody was hungry or thirsty. It was winter and there were built-in wall heaters around the factory to keep us warm.

My foreman was a German man in his forties with long, straight brown hair. One day soon after we arrived, he approached me.

"How old are you?" he asked. I wasn't sure why.

"Seventeen," I said.

"I have a daughter your age," he told me. He smiled. "Let me know how I can help you here. I will do as much as I can." I never learned his name; we just called him "Mister."

Even the Wehrmacht guards were civilized. A couple named Hildi and Fritz were in charge. They were boyfriend and girlfriend in their early twenties. They didn't try to intimidate us or scare us. They were cheerful and smiled. They reminded us that the end of the war was near and they encouraged us to be strong so we could all make it.

Their gentle kindness—the foreman's and Hildi and Fritz's—helped renew my faith in people. Klari felt the same way. We smiled. They smiled back. They treated us like human beings and that changed them in our eyes, too. I came to think of them not as Germans but simply as people.

I worked the night shift—from 3:30 p.m. until midnight. At first I had to adjust to that schedule and I would get very sleepy at night.

"Take a nap," the foreman said one night. "I'll wake you up if I need to."

We took regular showers and they served us decent food: cheese sandwiches, egg sandwiches.

The foreman would bring his lunch, and one day I watched him pull it out of his lunch box: a hard-boiled egg, hot chocolate, and a beautiful, red tomato.

Seeing that, I was suddenly transported back to our garden in Putnok and I felt overcome with emotion. I began to cry.

"What's wrong?" he asked.

"I'm sorry," I said. "It's the first tomato I've seen since I left Hungary."

I told him about our garden, and how Mother would take me with her and give me a basket to pick tomatoes; how she would pick tomatoes and put them in the pockets of her half-apron, wipe one off on her apron and offer it to me. I would tell her I didn't like them warm. But I would watch her take a bite and love it. Once I tasted one she brought and didn't like the taste in my mouth. "It's yucky! It's hot!" I said. I liked tomatoes cool, sliced in a salad. I thought that day about how many times Mother had offered me tomatoes and I didn't take them.

The foreman reached into his lunch box and pulled something out.

"Here, take one." It was a tomato—nice and cool. I took one bite and it felt like a *mechaya*, a miracle. Nothing had ever tasted so good. And I cried. I felt suddenly connected to Mother—and so sorry for all the times I hadn't listened to her and eaten tomatoes.

I thanked him.

"When I get home," I told him, "I'm going to have a tomato every day. And I will never forget you."

From then on, he would bring me tomatoes. I ate one every day.

Klari, who was still with me, felt the same way I did: It was a shock to be in a place where we were treated like human beings. One day I had a toothache. I thought it might be a gum infection. My face became swollen and I told the foreman.

In Auschwitz I had lived in fear of showing any weakness or pain. But here I felt more secure.

"Come on with me," he said. He led me to his car. I sat in the rear, lying down to avoid being seen. He could certainly face trouble if he were caught doing this.

It was late afternoon. He drove me about 10 minutes into the city to a dentist's office. The dentist sat me down and looked in my mouth. He drilled my tooth and gave me a filling, which fixed the problem. Again, it struck me. I thought: *God really loves me.*

I WAS 17 YEARS OLD, a developing adolescent. At Augsburg, I began to notice the man whose job was to check all the machines to make sure they were working properly. He was a French man named André, very cute and handsome and always smiling a big smile. No matter how bad the situation, a male is still a male and a female is a female. And he spoke some German. I saw all the other girls getting their chances to chat and laugh with André. I would watch him from three or four machines away. And I wanted my turn. I just thought he was so adorable. But my machine worked perfectly.

I didn't know how to fix my machine, but I figured out how to break it; I could adjust it so that it wouldn't produce the right size screws.

I called out, "André! André! Machine *kopput!*"

He finally came over. "*Ya, Ya, Ya,*" he said.

He took his tool, he tightened the machine and it was fixed.

I did that a few times, sabotaged my own machine just to get him to come over. After a while he noticed that I was cute, and we started having conversations. We really took a liking to each other and I didn't have to ruin my machine anymore to get him to come and chat.

One day he brought me a gift: he had taken a piece of metal with a small hole in it and carved his name on it. He put it on a string and gave it to me, along with a small photograph of himself.

"For you to remember me," André said.

I kept that small charm for many years.

AS SAFE AS I FELT AT AUGSBURG, there were dangers lurking. Once the belt of my uniform was hanging a bit too loosely and got caught in one of the other machines. I bent over and a hook caught the belt and suddenly pulled me up, over the top of the machine and slammed me hard onto the floor. I was knocked unconscious.

"Stop the machine!" the foreman was shouting. "Unplug the machine!"

Someone pulled the plug and I lay there unconscious. When I awoke, a crowd was surrounding me. Everyone was wondering if I was alive. I had a terrible headache. They took me to a doctor, who said I had suffered a concussion. I was lucky. If they hadn't unplugged the machine, I could have easily been killed.

The foreman was so concerned that they then rearranged the area so that the machines weren't so close together and nobody would get hurt. After that, every morning they would remind us to be careful—and always to tighten our belts securely.

They took care of us, one human being to another.

It showed most in how they treated one girl who was pregnant. She was one of three sisters from a very religious Jewish community in the city of Dunaszerdahely. She had been pregnant when they left Hungary, and somehow they let her carry her baby. The guards from Augsburg took her somewhere—maybe the Teresienstadt or Dachau camps, I never learned where—and she delivered the baby. And miraculously, she returned to the factory with her newborn. That was unheard of—a Jewish infant born in the midst of this nightmare.

THE WORK WAS DIFFICULT, but for five months, I experienced a respite in the midst of the storm. Then, one afternoon in April, the foreman gathered us together on the factory floor.

"I have news," he told us. "The Russian army is closing in on Germany. We can't stay here."

We were stunned. But it was a matter of survival. The German officers and workers didn't want to risk being captured or killed by the Russians. They wanted to save themselves—and, in turn, save us.

I shuddered at the idea of leaving Augsburg—for where? Where could we possibly go that would offer the same kind of refuge? Did this mean we were headed back to Auschwitz? Or to some other death factory? I cried, and so did Klari and all of the other girls. We simply didn't want to leave.

We had no choice. So we packed what little we had: our factory clothes and some food in backpacks they gave us. Together, we walked from the factory to the Augsburg railroad station and boarded a small passenger train. God knew where they were going to take us. Again, I was thrust back into the worst part of these terrifying months: the unknown.

10

Freedom

THE WAR WAS IN ITS FINAL DAYS, and those weeks were marked by confusion and desperation. We traveled for a day. When the train stopped, we all got off and walked, following the guards, for about half an hour. We arrived at Dachau, the concentration camp. We all waited—hundreds of us—while the Wermacht guards talked to SS men at the entrance. Then we got word that we couldn't stay. The Russian army was closing in and they were liquidating the camp. The Germans didn't want to take in new inmates. I didn't know if that news was good or bad. We stayed a couple of hours. They gave us soup and water. We waited to see if they would change their minds and let us in. But they refused.

They marched us back to the train station and we got back on a train.

After a short time we got off again, this time at Kaufering—one of Dachau's smaller subcamps. But this part of Kaufering was a men's camp. We stayed for two days. At this point, our guards simply didn't know what do with the hundreds of Jews in our camp. The more time that passed, the more disorder set in. The guards at Kaufering told our guards that no women would be allowed there. With nowhere to go, we slept on the grass outside the gates in a huge yard. We stayed

107

two days.

They piled us back on a train. Again, the ride was not long. We stopped in Mühldorf, another satellite camp of Dachau. Mühldorf was absorbing many prisoners who had come from different camps and they took us in. They put us to work harvesting potatoes. (Some of the girls worked in the kitchen, or sewing patches onto clothing.)

It was spring, the rainy season, and the rains were heavy that year. Spending so much time outside in the damp conditions, I started to get very sick. I had a high fever and a terrible rash on most of my body. I grew more and more weak and tired. And I knew why: I had contracted typhus. It was extremely contagious and many of the other girls also had also caught it. I was dehydrated and the fever kept soaring. Klari was sick, too.

Still, I had to work. We were back in a place with SS men in charge and it was like Auschwitz: They had no use for Jews who couldn't work. If they saw prisoners lying around they would not hesitate to take them out and shoot them. I was losing strength by the day, but I did my best to look strong.

After we had been at Mühldorf for two weeks, on April 15, 1945, they told us we had to leave; the American army was closing in. But there were no trains.

Speaking in a megaphone, one of the SS men issued the orders: "Get in a line," he said, "and start walking."

It felt like devastating news. I was in terrible condition—weak, delirious, burning up with a fever. I was thirsty and hungry but couldn't hold down food. Klari was suffering from the same illness. She was weak and getting weaker. But we followed orders. We lined up, and the Germans followed in their Jeeps and cars as we walked.

The walk seemed endless. On the road, I kept looking back behind me. So many people just couldn't keep up. They simply collapsed on the road and the Germans left them to die. And I quickly came to realize that that was their objective: If they hadn't killed us in our homes, if they hadn't suffocated us on the cattle cars, if they hadn't murdered us with gas and incinerated our bodies, if they hadn't worked us to death or driven us to suicide or shot us at will—if they hadn't succeeded at any of those, it would come to this. They would starve us and walk us until we simply could not go on. There was one destination: death.

I kept walking as all around me people grew weak and dropped, falling on the roadside.

"That's what's going to happen to us," I told Klari. "I can't go on too much longer."

This time she was the one to offer reassurance.

"We can't give up now," Klari said. "We have suffered so much. But it's going to come to an end."

We held on to each other on that long road, somewhere in Germany. (We had become separated from the Koth sisters.) During the day we walked. At night they ordered us to stretch out on the roadside. Spring rains kept falling. My clothes were soaked and my shoes—high, laced shoes I had been given at the factory—were giving out.

It was a miracle any of us were still alive.

They gave us no food or water. I pulled weeds to eat. We caught butterflies, insects from the trees—anything we could find or catch. We picked wild mushrooms. We chewed on grass. I was so ill, I didn't even feel hungry anymore, but I was thirsty. The Germans rode beside us on bicycles and jeeps and station wagons. We walked for hours at a time and then they would order us to sit down.

We got soaked by the rain, then the sun came up and dried our clothes. My shoes became caked in mud and grew heavier, even as my legs became weaker.

But we kept going.

One day I was so thirsty. I thought I would die. We were sitting on the roadside waiting for the Germans to tell us to get up and walk again.

"*Bitte, wasser,*" I begged. "*Bitte! Bitte!*"

The SS man laughed at me—a heavy, hard laugh. The guards were drinking beer and milk and hot chocolate. And we were starving.

Finally I was so dehydrated I could not even move my tongue in my mouth. We licked each other's perspiration to get fluid. Then I had no choice: I squatted, put my hands down, and collected my own urine in my palms. And I drank the fluid. It tasted salty and warm. Others did the same thing. We had long gowns and people just urinated in their cupped hands and drank it. We wanted to survive. I did that a few times.

I weighed probably 65 lbs. But I just kept praying that if I could hold on and live, I would be liberated.

As we walked, our group began merging with others who had been marching from other directions. And then on the last day of April, weak and barely alive, I spotted a sign of hope: Some of the German guards began taking off their uniforms, stripping to their t-shirts and tank-tops. Others were dropping their guns.

Dozens of airplanes were flying over. It was noisy and chaotic.

I saw some of the guards take prison garb from prisoners and put it on, attempting to look like prisoners. Of course, they didn't and couldn't. They looked healthy and well nourished and we all looked like skeletons. But they wanted to look like prisoners—because they knew the American army was getting close.

Finally, it was a ray of hope. I had lived this long. And I knew I could make it.

The next morning, May 1, 1945, there was a beautiful sunrise. At around 4 a.m. a tank appeared on the road. In the still dim light, I noticed it was flying a flag—different from any we had seen. I squinted, trying to make it out as the tank got closer. Then I realized: It was an American flag.

I was weak and had almost no energy left. But I felt a surge of joy and relief I had never before experienced as the tank slowed and came to a stop near us.

Soldiers got out, healthy-looking men who looked up and down the lines, taking in the sight: hundreds of prisoners, emaciated, weak, near death. I watched their faces and their horrified expressions. They kept looking at us and saying things in English I didn't understand.

"Oh my God!" they were saying, and looking at each other. "Look at these people!"

I could tell from their expressions that they were stunned. But they tried to bring us some comfort—to make us understand what had happened,

"Baby, you're gonna be okay!" they kept saying to me. "Baby, you're gonna be okay!"

Others kept repeating: "You're free!"

Some were shouting: "Freedom, freedom!"

That much I understood.

They threw us Hershey bars and American cigarettes. They had canned food. They hauled out everything they had. They gave us water from their canteens.

Another day and I might have been dead. But I suddenly regained my strength. Weak as we were, we all jumped up and down with joy.

One soldier approached the area where I was standing with Klari.

"Kenst du redn Yiddish?" he asked—Who speaks Yiddish?

I raised my hand and went closer.

"I speak Yiddish," I told him, my voice so faint it was barely audible.

He said he was from the Bronx, New York. And he was Jewish. I looked at this man: he was about my own age, medium height, with a dark complexion and big grin. In all of these months, it was the first time I had met a Jew with the power to help us. Then he told us in Yiddish what the others had been trying to say in English.

"You're free," he told us. He explained we were going to get help from doctors and they would get us medicine.

"We're going to take care of you," he said.

He told us they would take us to a displaced persons camp.

Then the soldier looked me up and down, looked me in the eye and made a request.

"Point a finger at the one who made you look like a skeleton."

Some of the Germans were standing nearby. Yiddish is similar to German. I'm sure they understood. I was shaking, and the soldier touched my shoulder.

"Just relax, you're okay," he said. "You're free."

He waited for me to answer. I looked around him, at the soldiers—stunned and speechless—and at faces of the dozens of other Jews

111

around me, all gaunt, weak and just clinging to life. I could hear gunfire echoing in the woods. I took a breath.

"I want to go home with a clear conscience," I told him. "I don't want to hurt anybody."

"Are you *meshuggeh?*" he asked. "Look at yourself! You're crazy! Look how you look! Look what they did to you!"

I thought of Father.

"I come from a religious family," I told him. "My father always taught me what the Talmud says: 'If you save one life, it is as if you have saved the whole world.'"

He listened in silence. I continued.

"I know they deserve to be punished," I said. "But I don't want to participate. I don't want to be part of it. I just want to go home. I don't want to harm anyone. They deserve it, but they're human beings. Every soldier must be somebody's father or husband or son."

The officer looked at me, still waiting.

"The war is over," I said. "I want to go home."

All around us, I could hear other prisoners screaming and shouting.

"Death to the Germans!" they cried. "Death to all of them!"

I did not join in.

"I just want to go home," I said.

Emaciated people in prison garb were converging from all directions. They had all seen the tanks and the American flags. People were cheering. They were limping and holding on to each other, carrying each other, clinging to life and trying to join the liberators.

By then the Nazi guards had fled. They were all over the forest around us. They knew that if they were caught, they would be held as prisoners of war—or worse. From the dark of the woods, I heard shots ringing out. I knew Americans were facing German troops, who were now greatly outnumbered.

I didn't want to be part of that. I just wanted to go home.

They took us to a makeshift hospital nearby in Feldafing, just outside Munich. The complex had been a training compound for Hitler Youth. The Nazi uniforms were strewn across the floors—as if the men had quickly shed their uniforms and fled. The Germans were all gone. And we were moving in.

IN THE MIDST OF THAT NOISY, chaotic rush came a miraculous, transcendent moment. As we approached the compound where we were to take refuge, we had to trudge through a muddy field. Klari and I walked together, holding hands. Near the entrance, I took a step and suddenly I felt something under my foot—something jutting from the ground. I paused and looked down. Suddenly something rose up out of the mud and I realized what it was: a human hand.

Oh my God, I thought. *I'm walking on a human being.*

The hand was slowly moving, so I realized the person must be alive. Klari and I knelt down to look more closely. I grasped the hand, dug another from the mud and grasped the two hands, holding on, and not knowing whose hands I was holding. Klari ran and found a hose nearby to wash off the mud. Bit by bit, it washed away, revealing a face. It was a middle-aged man. I bent down to get a closer look, taking in the sight. And then I realized: I knew this man.

It was Mr. Lovy, my father's close friend from Putnok. He was the nephew of the man who had sat next to me on the cattle car—the one Mother and I had helped.

He was practically unconscious, so he didn't recognize me. He just kept muttering and praying to God. *"Shema Yisroel! Shema Yisroel!"*

Klari washed him off and hosed off his arms. We tried to pull him up. We were both weak and frail but we each grabbed an arm and we pulled him up. We walked—Klari holding one hand, I the other, and we carried him that way into the compound. We found a room and a bed for him and lay him down.

After a while, he had a few sips of water and rested and gradually began to come to. I stood over his bed and he blinked and looked at me.

"Mr. Lovy!" I said. "I'm Shloyme Rosenfeld's daughter!"

"God bless you!" he kept saying. *"Shemisborach* is with me!"

He was barely alive. He held his head up and we gave him more water to sip. He was so weak. Back in Putnok, Mr. Lovy ran a salt factory and he had daughters older than I was. I wondered what Father would think if he could see this—that I had carried Mr. Lovy from the mud and saved his life!

I made sure he got hot soup.

"Eat slowly," I kept telling him.

In the makeshift hospital, we found Mr. Lovy a change of clothing and shoes. Later we carried him outside into the sun to get some air. As weak and frail as I felt, now I had someone else to care for, someone who embodied so much of what I had lost. In that moment of redemption, I felt like I had found my father.

DOCTORS ARRIVED. An American Jewish chaplain came and gave us encouragement. An army with a Jewish chaplain!

They set up a kitchen. I knew I had to eat slowly. I watched others who had been so hungry for so very long; they couldn't stop themselves. They ate whatever they could get their hands on quickly. Their systems were overwhelmed. And some of them couldn't take it. The shock to their bodies killed them.

At first I just drank water—then, finally, I tried a biscuit.

I ate slowly, just one bite at a time. I was hardly able to chew. Later, they brought us soup, juice, bread, canned food.

Some of the foods were unfamiliar—U.S. Army rations. It was the first time I had seen Heinz half-peaches or baked beans.

They brought us silverware. It was heaven.

I just prayed. I just kept thanking God that I was alive. They left me alone with Klari, who looked as bad as I did, so thin and weak she was like a skeleton.

I took a hot shower. That felt great. And I lay down to rest.

It was a beautiful day. We opened the windows and we sat looking out, taking in the sunshine.

Over the next three weeks, I ate slowly—a tiny bit more at a time—and rested. I started feeling better. I planned my life.

One morning I woke up and looked in the mirror and saw that my hair was starting to grow back. My face was filling out. And I began to see the young woman who had left Putnok eleven months earlier. I looked like a human being—like a woman should.

For weeks I had been wearing my prison gown. But now I couldn't wait to get out of it. (I washed it in a lake nearby and wore a bed sheet while I waited for it to dry.) I looked at my mattress and took some scissors and ripped off the mattress cover—a blue and white checkered fabric. I asked for a needle and thread. I started sewing a dress, stitch by stitch—my first dress. I had never learned to sew, but I felt like I was the best-dressed woman in the world.

Among all the white officers and soldiers, there was one black man. I had never seen a black person in my life—except in the movies. He was huge in size and, it turned out, had a huge heart.

"Who is that person?" we kept asking a translator.

It was scary, in a way, when you're not used to a different ethnicity. He said he was from Youngstown, Ohio. I knew where Ohio was, but not Youngstown. He told us he had been separated from the black unit—the U.S. army was segregated—and he had joined the white officers. He couldn't drive a car. He walked into Munich—two kilometers from Feldafing—and brought milk and biscuits for us. We were getting enough food, but he wanted us to have something special.

Over the days, I came to love his pleasant and reassuring presence.

"I don't have a sister," he told me one day, "but when I'm ready to go home, I want to take you with me." He was joking, but he said it with such charm and wit. "My mother would love to have a daughter like you!"

"You're an angel," I told him. I had always thought of angels as having ivory skin and blue eyes and blond hair. But this was an angel. And we kept calling him our guardian angel. If people had trouble walking, he would get them a cane and help them. (Now I speak to audiences of many different ethnicities—blacks, Mexicans, Indians, Asians—and I've gotten to know people different from me. And I often tell that story. I didn't get his name. I never thought there would be a time that I'd be able to tell people about him.)

While we were in Feldafing, Fritz and Hilda—the couple from the factory—were there. They had driven with the Germans during the March. We made sure to tell the Americans how wonderful they had been. They had made sure we were treated humanely and that we got food, that no one was harmed. (Not long after I left Feldafing, I heard that they got married. One of the chaplains from the American army performed the ceremony and everyone danced. Some of my friends were still there.)

The officer from the Bronx I had met the first day kept returning. And others came with interpreters.

"Where do you want to go?" he would ask. "Canada? Sweden? A displaced persons camp?" They would take us wherever we wanted. They wanted to help us get to wherever we needed to go.

I had only one desire, and I told him: I just wanted to go home to Hungary—and so did Klari. We had to see if we could find our families and friends.

The officer said he could take us as far as Czechoslovakia, and from there we could take the train.

In late May, three weeks after our arrival, 50 of us girls loaded into eight or ten jeeps. It was a day's drive to Prague. When we got there, we stopped at a large restaurant. The chef came out and asked everybody what their favorite foods were. I asked him to make me poppy seed noodles, scrambled eggs and coffee. It all tasted delicious.

But what I really hungered for was home. I had no idea who from my family was still alive, or where they might be. I was desperate to find some clue.

We walked to a building not far from there that had been a Jewish school. They had rooms for us to stay. We moved in and I took a hot shower. Prague was a ruined city from all the bombing. Some of the girls wanted to see the city, but I didn't want to see anything.

I just wanted to get home.

In the building lobby I noticed the walls were lined with posters, a mass of hundreds of handwritten signs in different languages—Polish, Czech, Hungarian—tacked to the wall. There must have been 500 notes from people who had passed through and left words in case their loved ones were trying to find them.

I started searching, knowing there was little chance of finding anything helpful in this mess of papers. Just as I started looking—I had looked at only four or five of the hundreds of messages—my eyes were drawn directly to something just at my eye level: my father's handwriting!

Solomon Rosenfeld.
I passed through in January
and I am heading back to Putnok.

There were hundreds of slips of paper and here was my father's beautiful writing in the first few I read! It was a miracle!

Oh my God! I thought, *Father is alive! We have to get out of here!*

"Let's get out of Prague," I told Klari. "Let's go home."

11

The World That Remained

CHAOS REIGNED IN PRAGUE, and looters were ransacking homes where Germans had been living, making off with cameras or paintings—whatever they could find. I watched ordinary people carrying off beautiful pillows and embroidered blankets. I stayed away. I didn't need possessions. I didn't need to take anything. All I needed was what little I had: my mattress-cover dress, the pair of sandals someone had given me in the makeshift hospital and a single brown blanket the American soldiers had given me.

I just wanted to leave.

I put some rolls, cheese, fruit, and water in a canvas bag and Klari and I walked to the railroad station. It was packed with all kinds of people: soldiers and travelers and peasants selling goods. We found the platform for the train to Budapest and found the conductor, who spoke Hungarian.

"When is the train leaving?" I asked.

"Soon," he said.

Klari and I looked at him.

"Can we get on?" I asked.

"There's no room," he said. He said the train was just too crowded. I looked up and down the platform. He was right; each train had a sign: FULL, FULL, FULL.

"Wait for the next train," he said.

"The next one will be full, too," I said.

I looked up and I saw soldiers bracing themselves to ride atop some of the cars. So I appealed to him for some mercy.

"I can't wait," I said. "I just found out my father is alive. He's home waiting for me." I told him we had just been liberated and I hadn't seen my father in a year. "If there are no seats, will you let us ride on the roof of the train?"

"Are you crazy? It's too dangerous," he said. "You survived all of that. Don't risk your life doing this."

"Look, there are soldiers up there!" I said.

"They're soldiers," he said. "You're just a kid."

I looked him in the eye. "Help us get there," I said.

Finally, he relented and helped us to climb up. We used wire and rope to secure ourselves on top of the car just behind the locomotive.

"Say a prayer," he said. "This may not be so safe."

The train started to move and thick, black smoke was billowing out of the engine. My stomach was shaking. None of that concerned me at all. We covered ourselves with blankets but before long, the thick smoke enveloped us. I looked at Klari and everything but her teeth and eyeballs were black and sooty. I didn't have a mirror, but I knew I must have looked the same way.

The train traveled slowly—the trainmen were wary of landmines near the tracks—and when it stopped at night, Klari and I loosened the ropes and stretched out to rest. Then at daybreak, it started moving again and we secured the ropes and sat up.

After two days' journey, we pulled into Budapest. I saw the name of the station: KELETI PLYAUDVAR. The Russians were occupying Hungary, so I immediately saw a lot of Russian soldiers. But the signs were all in Hungarian. Being back in my own country, I felt a rush of warmth and comfort combined with a sense of dread and loss for how drastically my life had changed since I had left Hungary in a very different train 11 months earlier.

The conductor untied us. Klari and I clambered down the ladder and stood on the platform. We both kissed the ground—to be back in the land of our birth! I said a prayer to thank God for getting us there.

The station was busy and as crowded as you can imagine. I saw a group of Jews. The Jewish Agency had organized to have groups of Jews in every major railroad station in Europe to help survivors connect, to give them money and encouragement.

"Who are you?" they were asking. "Where do you want to go?"

I recognized one of the men: Mr. Birinbaum—Sanya Birinbaum from one of the large Jewish families in Putnok.

"I'm Eva Rosenfeld," I told him. "I know who you are."

"Reb Shloyme's daughter!" he said in Yiddish. "Oh my God! What happened to you?"

I remembered my face was covered with soot. I explained that I had been traveling for two days atop a train.

"You need a good scrub," he said. And then he gave me news: "Your father is alive." My eyes welled up. For a year I had worried and fretted about my father's fate, always fearing the worst but praying for the best. He was alive.

"I'll take you to him," Mr. Birinbaum said.

I was in heaven. I asked Klari if she wanted to come with me. But Klari had some relatives and friends in Budapest. She wanted to make contact with them. She didn't want to go home. We said goodbye. "We'll find each other," she said. It was the first time we had separated since that first day in Auschwitz when we found ourselves pushed away from our families, in the same horrible line. It was difficult to separate, but it was what we had to do.

I got cleaned up, took a hot shower, got new clothes and money and more food. I wanted to save the blanket and my mattress-cover dress—I just needed keepsakes; I had so little. I put it all in my canvas bag.

Mr. Birinbaum drove me to the city of Miskolc. On the four-hour drive, he shared with me the news of Father: He had come home in January to Putnok. Father had been very run down and he found only 17 Jews in all of Putnok. He needed to be hospitalized, so Mr. Birinbaum had taken him to Miskolc. While he was in the hospital, a rabbi who was a professor, a Dr. Klein, visited him and invited Father to come stay at his home when Father was well enough to leave the hospital. Mr. Birinbaum told me that in March, when Father had recovered, he moved into Dr. Klein's house and joined in the effort to organize kitchens and hospitals for the survivors. Now they had a kosher kitchen near the shul and a small daily minyan. They began to build a community.

It was early June. A Thursday, late in the afternoon. Mr. Birinbaum drove me to the address in Miskolc: No. 4 Mindszenty. It was a very large house with a huge, beautiful garden. I knocked on the door and my heart raced while I waited for someone to come to the door. When it opened, I was greeted by a small man with a gray beard and a large black yarmulke.

"Rabbi Klein?" I asked.

"Yes."

I told him who I was.

"Your father is fine," he said. "He's in shul. He should be back soon. Would you like to wait for him inside?" I told him I would wait outside. The house had a large patio. I sat down. I kept my eyes glued to the large wooden gate. It was almost dark, but I wanted to see him as soon as he came. I wanted to seize the moment.

While I waited, I pondered what I could possibly say to Father. I had not seen him in a year, and all that time I'd had no way of knowing about his fate, his health, what dangers he was facing—even whether he was alive. How many times I had prayed for his life and health. Now what could I possibly say? I tried to compose the sentences. *"I'm so glad you're here."* I tried to imagine the conversation.

And then I spotted him, coming up the street from shul. It was Father, but he was different—thin, and seemingly many years older. His black beard had turned white. He looked like a broken, sad man. When he saw me, he embraced me and said a prayer. He offered a Hebrew blessing and said the *Shehechianu*—the prayer thanking God for sustaining us in life. He didn't say a word to me—he couldn't— and I couldn't say a word to him. We each had a lump in our throat. I felt a heaviness, a pain I cannot describe.

Father had been so strong: He was a war hero, he led a community, he raised seven children, he went to forced labor, to a concentration camp, and here we were facing each other. We were speechless.

We went inside. He pulled out a white handkerchief, tied its corners, placed it tenderly on my head, and offered another blessing. He lit a candle, and opened up his *siddur*. I sat down. He prayed and the candle burned. I felt so weak. Seeing him took some of the life out of me. I watched him as he prayed and prayed, for an hour or two. I wasn't hungry. I wasn't thirsty. Finally, I spoke.

"Dad," I said. "Talk to me. There's so much to say."

"There's not much good I can tell you," he said, "Our life is never going to be the same again. It's going to be an imitation of life. Whatever it was, it's over."

He told me he knew what had happened to Mother and the children at Auschwitz; by then everyone had heard what happened at the death camps—how the Nazis had murdered and cremated the mothers and grandmothers and the young children. He didn't have to ask me.

He told me about my brother Andor, who had been in a forced labor camp. Andor contracted tetanus and died. (Later we would learn exactly how.)

My two older sisters, Irene and Aranka, had been taken away from Budapest. He had heard they were both in the Bergen-Belsen camp but they had survived.

My younger brother, Sandor, was alive, too. He had posed as a member of the Arrow Cross, the Hungarian SS troupe, using his hidden identity to save the lives of hundreds of Jews the authorities had condemned to death. After the Russians came into Hungary, his picture had been posted all over Budapest on lampposts and store windows; he was wanted as an Arrow Cross member and had escaped to Italy. He was one of thousands of Jews who obtained papers from Raoul Wallenberg, the Swedish diplomat, helping them to pass as gentiles.

Father told me two of my uncles had survived, one from my mother's side and one from my father's.

Of the 67 people in our extended family, seven had survived.

We stayed up all night. There was more silence than talking. He prayed. We sat. The candle burned.

Finally the sun was starting to rise. "Leah," he told me, "I have to get ready to go to shul. We'll have breakfast when I come back. We have to rest up and then make a plan and wait for everyone to come home."

IN THE SUCCEEDING DAYS AND WEEKS, Father and I traveled to nearby villages seeking out Jews who had been hidden by Hungarian families—in stables, in attics and basements, in churches. It was his way of continuing his work as a community leader. A lot of people were still hiding. When the Russians had arrived, many of these hidden Jews had been afraid to emerge, fearing they would be hurt. Father traveled the country, trying to gather them. And he went to the shuls to see if there remained any Torah scrolls or prayer books or other sacred Jewish texts. He found very little. The Nazis had destroyed so much.

We traveled together to Köszeg, the city where my brother Andor, the cantor, had died. Someone who had been with him in the forced labor camp there told us that Andor had been forced with other Jewish men to jump into the icy Danube river and then he had developed a tetanus infection. He grew weaker and more sickly, and one Saturday evening, as the skies darkened, men gathered around as he sang *Got Fun Avrohom*, a Yiddish prayer marking the end of Shabbat. They said Andor's voice, his great gift, faded more and more until he simply closed his eyes—and he was gone. They buried him in a mass grave.

One uncle, Moshe—Mother's brother—survived and returned to Hajdúböszörmény. (Mother's sister's husband came home much later.) When Father and I traveled there we visited the neighborhood where my grandparents had lived—where I had carried the *challah* for Zayde as a young girl. The survivors we found told us what little they knew: Even before they arrived at Auschwitz, my Grandmother Rivka had suffocated and died in a cattle car.

Later I learned that my grandfather, Zayde Yitzhak, had sent a final postcard to my sisters in Budapest in the last days of the ghetto in Hajúduböszörmény.

"I'm closing my home—I have to leave," he had written. "God bless the whole world." That was the last any of us had heard from him. My grandfather died at Auschwitz—along with uncles and cousins and others. We couldn't find any more relatives.

We had a cousin in Los Angeles. Father wrote to him that we were home. He wrote back, offering to help sponsor us and help us move to the United States. He encouraged us to sign up, but said that with quotas, it could take three years.

Another uncle, Father's brother Sheeya Rosenfeld, returned to Hajuszobszlo, the town my father came from. Father sent me there to spend the summer with another girl nursing Uncle Sheeya back to health. I was outside hanging laundry there one morning when suddenly I spotted someone running through the gate—a young man wearing a khaki shirt and shorts and a shielded hat. It was my brother Sandor!

"Shaya!" I said, using the Hebrew name I had always called him. He raced to me, held out his arms and embraced me as we both cried. It felt so bittersweet. I felt such relief to see him, but we both knew how much we had lost.

"What are you doing here?" I asked him.

He told me he had returned from Italy. First he had made his way to Budapest, where he had heard that Father was home. So he had gone to see Father, who told him that I was alive and with my uncle.

He had taken the train to see me.

"I'm not going to be in Hungary much longer," Sandor said. "I'm going to Palestine."

I was speechless. "You can't leave us—we need you," I told him. Of the seven of us, he was the only male child to survive. "Besides, Father will never let you go!"

"This is something I have to do," Sandor told me. "I have to go and build a Jewish state."

I went back to visit Father, and the three of us stayed there. I told Sandor to wait until our sisters returned—and then we could all make our decisions together. Father looked at Sandor.

"You're the only son I have," he said, "You are my *Kaddish*,"—the only son surviving to say the mourner's prayer for Father.

"I'll have to be your *Kaddish* in Palestine," Sandor said. "And maybe you'll come to Palestine."

"I'm too old," Father said. The idea of moving to a kibbutz and doing heavy labor to work the land was simply too much for him. He wanted to go to the United States, where he had a cousin who was a rabbi.

As for me, I wouldn't leave Father.

That September Irene and Aranka returned from Bergen-Belsen. They both looked like skeletons. They had sunken eyes. Their teeth were rotten. Their gums were in terrible shape. They both had suffered from typhus. Their voices were weak; they could hardly speak. Irene told us that Aranka had been near death; she had been literally carrying her around on her back. Then she had decided she couldn't return home alone. How would she tell her family she hadn't taken care of her own sister?

"God helped us," Irene said. They had made it home together.

Now we had a full house: Father, Aranka, Irene, Sandor and me. We had a room, and almost nothing else. Father found a folding table. Father told us that in the Jewish religion, only dead people sleep on the floor. We had a dresser with large drawers; Father pulled out the drawers and put blankets in. One sister slept on top of the dresser and another sister and I—we were so tiny—we each slept in a drawer. Father slept on a cot he had picked up somewhere. That was our home. We got food from a community kitchen.

Sandor stayed with us a year. He worked with the Mizrachi group, and in 1946 he fulfilled his dream and moved to Palestine. His ship was captured by the British and taken to Cyprus, where he stayed for a year. When Israel became a state in 1948, he arrived and volunteered for the new Israeli army.

Sandor had been there only about three months when he stepped on a landmine during the War of Independence. He died in July 1948. My brother—who survived so much, fought so hard, and fulfilled his dream of moving to Palestine—was buried in a military cemetery in Tel Aviv.

My sister Aranka got married in 1947. The tradition had always been that the oldest daughter married first. Aranka was the second oldest, and she apologized to Irene, the oldest. They both knew that if Mother had been alive, this never would have happened; Mother wouldn't have allowed it. But the life we knew was gone. Aranka and her husband Yosef supervised a Jewish youth group, the Mizrachi group. And that same year they went to Palestine with the Youth Aliyah. They settled in the Negev and had three children.

For many years I didn't know what had become of Klari. It was only in 1967 that I found her when I visited Israel. She was the only one in her family to survive. She had moved to Herzliya, Israel and was raising her six children. For years we spoke every May 1, recalling the joy of our liberation day.

Just two or three weeks after our reunion, Father and I went back to Putnok, to a wedding. Lenke Koth—the older of the two sisters from Putnok I had been with in Auschwitz—married her high school sweetheart, also from Putnok, and Father conducted the ceremony.

Together, we walked around town to see what remained. What we found at the synagogue was heartbreaking. I couldn't even step inside. I looked in through the window while Father went in. Everything was gone. It was empty. Vandals had torn out the seats and made off with the Torah scrolls and prayer books. Gypsies were living in the synagogue and using it as a pottery factory.

We found the cemetery in ruins, with tombstones overturned and overgrown grass.

WE WENT TO OUR HOUSE and found gypsies living there. Father told them, "This belongs to the Jewish community." But what did that mean anymore? Putnok's Jewish community had been destroyed. Jewish life was gone. Out of 250 Jewish families in the town, just 17 young people had returned. The others who had survived were in displaced persons camps, or had gone to Sweden to recover from tuberculosis or other diseases. From there, many went on to Canada or Israel or the United States.

Father and I had no interest in living in Putnok anymore. There just weren't enough people left.

Before we left, I wanted to find the neighbor, Pista Toth, who had tried to save my life when we were in the ghetto. But when I knocked on their door, only two of the family remained: Irene, the girl, and her father, who was a railroad executive. Irene was surprised to see us, and expressed it in an abrupt way.

"Leah!" she said, calling me by my Hebrew name. "Jesus Christ! I thought you were all dead! How come you're still alive!?"

She told me that both of her brothers had died fighting on the front line. When we had left for the ghetto, Mother had given the Toths a number of our household items for safekeeping. She still had one: a tablecloth I had embroidered at age 10 when Mother had decided I needed to start a trousseau. Irene gave it to me.

I took the tablecloth, but Father and I left Putnok behind, focusing our energies on Miskolc, which had a much larger Jewish community, with more Jews returning all the time. The young people were cleaning up the shuls, the schools, the neighborhoods. Jewish life was continuing. After four or five months we started celebrating weddings and bar mitzvahs—everything. Jewish life was renewing.

In January of 1947, I went to the wedding in Szikszó of a close friend's brother. It was a very cold day. Father was officiating as rabbi, but when he was ready to start, the groom's best friend hadn't arrived yet. Finally, he arrived—it was so cold his horse had had a hard time getting through the snow. I was sitting with the bride when a man came and joined me and introduced himself: It was Ernie Braun. He was bright and he had a good sense of humor. He had been in the Hungarian Army and survived Buchenwald. Like me, he had lost most of his family. We became friends almost instantly, and later that year, we married.

12

A New Life

NOT LONG AFTER I EMIGRATED to the United States—with Ernie, Father and Irene—I went to see a psychiatrist.

We had come in 1948 to Los Angeles, where Father had a sister and brother-in-law. It was a difficult transition. We arrived with seven dollars and almost no connections and spoke virtually no English.

I suffered all kinds of physical ailments: pain in my back and side and, often, painful stomach problems. Just walking down the street I would suddenly feel overwhelming nausea. Father saw me suffering and kept telling me I needed to see a doctor. He took me on the streetcar to Cedars of Lebanon Hospital in Hollywood (now Cedars-Sinai Medical Center), where indigent patients could pay just one quarter to see a doctor. The receptionist spotted my tattoo.

"Before you see a doctor," she said, "I want you to see a psychiatrist."

The Hungarian-speaking doctor happened to have an available appointment just then, at 1 p.m. I sat down in his office and he set down a water pitcher and a box of Kleenex.

"Just tell me what happened to you," he said. "Don't hold back."

For two and a half hours, I never stopped talking. And the one who used up the water and the Kleenex was the psychiatrist.

"That's enough," he finally said, "I get the picture." He reassured me. "You have a lot of work to do. But you're going to live to be a very strong old woman. If you lived through that, you will live through anything."

I asked when I could come back to tell him more, but he shook his head.

"I needed you more than you need me," he said. "I learned so much about how strong a human being can be."

X-rays revealed that my hardships had caused serious ailments: My small and large intestines were entangled, and over the years I would need eight surgeries to relieve my various gastrointestinal maladies, as well as gum problems that came from malnutrition and—I am certain—from drinking the awful water in Auschwitz.

It was three years before I returned to relatively good health.

JUST AS FATHER HAD BEEN A LOYAL Hungarian before the war, he became a patriotic American. He lived next door to us in Boyle Heights, then the Jewish section of Los Angeles, where he was one of three rabbis at the Breed Street Synagogue, the city's oldest temple. I was with him the day in 1952 when he became a citizen. At the immigration office, the officer looked him up and down, a man in his black suit and hat carrying an American flag and smiling.

"Rabbi, what have you got to say for yourself?" he said.

"God bless the United States," Father said.

He signed a form and was granted citizenship.

I was nearly nine months into my first pregnancy when Father died from a heart attack on Feb. 22, 1955—George Washington's Birthday. He was 62. The day of the funeral people lined up for blocks in the rain to pay tribute to their beloved rabbi.

I had lost my rock. But God is always bringing renewal. One week later, I gave birth to my first child, Nancy. Father had come to a baby shower for me and given us one hundred dollars to buy a crib. But he didn't live to see his grandchild.

Our second daughter, Sandy, was born in January of 1957.

As much as I wished I could give my daughters the kind of idyllic childhood I had experienced before the war, it was impossible. Times were different. Their grandparents were all gone, and we were still acclimating to a new country.

Ernie and I gave them a lot of love—sometimes too much. I was an overprotective mother, always keeping an eye on the girls. Because we had both lost so much, we didn't give them the sort of freedom other parents afforded their children. When they were young, I would move their playpen close to wherever I was—even in the bathroom or the kitchen—to keep a constant eye on them. Even when they were old enough to walk to school on their own, I would walk them nearly all the way, then stand on the corner waving until they were safely inside.

We also tried to protect them from the scars of our own past. Like most survivors of the Holocaust, Ernie and I avoided discussing our experiences for many years.

Just after the war, when we were still in Hungary, I had been reading a book by a survivor about the Nazis' medical experiments in Auschwitz when I told Father I wanted to write something recounting my experiences, but he quashed the thought.

"This should be erased from your memory," he told me. "You need to rebuild your life—not live in the past."

Ernie had the same attitude. I respected his desire to remain silent. It was so personal. All of us who survived came away with unique perspectives. Who could tell someone else how to cope?

Instead, we focused on making a livelihood. Ernie—who had been a lawyer in Hungary—worked as a supervisor for the city of Los Angeles's animal-control department and I raised the girls and then got work at the Los Angeles County Library and, after that, the Beverly Hills Public Library.

My past would sometimes find me. In the late 1970s I was at the Los Angeles German consulate when a woman approached me. After Germany began paying compensation to Holocaust survivors in 1968, I had begun dutifully reporting to the consulate annually to present my identification as proof that I was still alive and eligible for my payment. I was in a line there when a middle-aged woman with a thick Polish accent recognized me.

"You're the Hungarian Eva!" she said in Yiddish.

She did not look familiar.

"How do you know me?" I asked.

"From Auschwitz," she said. She was from the Polish city of Lodz and we had never met. "You were always smiling. You had such beautiful white teeth. Nobody smiles like you."

It had been four decades. We had never spoken, but she remembered my smile.

"I always wondered," she said. "How could you always smile in Auschwitz?"

I told her it was just something I felt I needed to do to stay alive.

The truth is that I smiled when people were around me. But when I was alone—when nobody could see—I cried. I cried as much as I smiled in Auschwitz. When everyone else was asleep at night, I lay in my bunk and sobbed. But never in front of others. Never in front of the guards. And never near my friends.

I am certain that helped me survive. I'm sure it also helped the others around me to keep going, as best they could.

OCCASIONALLY I WOULD SEE BOOKS at the library about the Holocaust. I would flip through the pages and feel so upset that I would just put the book away. Colleagues, with the best of intentions, would set aside books on the war for me. One showed me a children's book about youths arriving at the Teresienstadt camp. When I saw it, I became so upset I felt ill. Suddenly I had an awful headache. I told my supervisor I didn't feel well; I had to go home. It brought back such awful memories.

Every year, June was particularly traumatic. For years, I would wake up with a jolt on June 13—the anniversary of the day I boarded the cattle car in Diosgyör. For two days, I would hear that haunting sound: the incessant rattling of the train, as if I were back there again. For 48 hours, the infernal sound would follow me—even as I tried to go about my life in Los Angeles—and then suddenly stop. It was so rooted in my bloodstream that it would come back, year after year, on that same date to torment me.

I told a doctor about the problem, appealing to him for help ridding my mind of the disturbing, upsetting noise. He suggested I try hypnosis. He said it might help expel the sounds from my memory. But he warned that in the process, I might lose other memories—even memories I held precious.

"No," I told him. "I don't want to forget anything—except for that sound."

I had read that the best way to overcome the memory of an accident or any awful experience is to return to the scene. So, many years later, Ernie and I returned to Hungary to attend the 1984 ceremonies commemorating the fortieth anniversary of the deportations. We rented a car in Budapest and drove to Diosgyör.

On June 13, 1984—exactly 40 years from the day I had boarded the cattle car with my mother and siblings—we arrived in Diosgyör. The weather was the same as it had been. The town hadn't changed much. Near the station, we saw railroad cars lined up, loaded with cows and horses, ready to ship. I stood there watching, frozen.

"My God," I said. "These are the cars we rode to Auschwitz." Not the exact cars, of course, but they looked the same. And they were on the same tracks. I took out a memorial candle and lit it. Ernie walked away and I stood in silence. I stayed there at least an hour. The memories flooded back. I stood there reliving what had happened, those awful days when Father had been taken, when the remnants of our community had been shoved into those cramped cars. I closed my eyes and pictured the scene: Mr. Lovy, the starving babies, the corpses.

Ernie strolled back to where I stood and said it was time to go; we'd been there long enough. I told him I wanted to sit in the cattle car. He talked me out of it. Enough, he said.

A year later, when June 13 came, the sound was gone.

I still visualized the scene. But I had expelled that ghastly sound from my system. It didn't take a psychiatrist. I had done it myself—one more step in reclaiming my life.

13

Without Hatred

WHEN THE GIRLS WERE YOUNG, they came to understand intui-
tively that we had secrets, and occasionally they would ask
questions. Why didn't they have grandparents? Why didn't they have
cousins? But we simply weren't ready to talk about it.

Nancy was five when she started asking about my tattoo.

I knew someday I would tell her. She was simply too young. I
didn't want to upset her. And where would I even begin?

But children have ways of finding the truth. One evening, when
Nancy was 10 or 11, she misplaced her eyeglasses and was searching
for them everywhere in the house. When she looked under our bed,
she found a copy of *Life* magazine Ernie had hidden there. That issue
carried dramatic, chilling photographs from Auschwitz. Nancy snuck
the magazine to her room to read it. Of course, she had always sensed
that her parents were somehow different—that we had a dark and
secret past. And now she came to perceive some of what we had survived. Perhaps that also helped her to understand why we had been
so overly protective of her.

When she was 12, Nancy's Girl Scout troop invited me to speak
about my past. It was the first time I had spoken publicly about my
experience and I spoke only briefly. I told them about my childhood,

about Hungary's oppressive laws, and about how we had all been deported. Even though I talked only briefly, the experience proved traumatic for both of us.

"Mom," Nancy said, "I think I've heard enough."

I didn't speak publicly again for more than 20 years, when my granddaughter invited me to address her high school class. Other than that, I kept my story to myself.

Then came *Schindler's List*. Steven Spielberg's 1993 film was the first I had seen that felt true to my own experiences. It felt authentic and real. It proved cathartic, and I felt ready to tell of my own story. When Spielberg's Survivors of the Shoah Foundation began recording testimonies, I immediately volunteered to tell my story. An interviewer and cameraman came to our home to interview me on videotape. Ernie wanted no part of it. While I spoke to the interviewer in the living room, Ernie lingered in the back of the house.

It was painful and difficult, but it also felt like a sacred task. At last I was carrying out that promise I had made in Auschwitz.

ERNIE DIED OF CANCER in October of 1997, and in 2001, I retired from the library. I wanted to stay active so I volunteered at two institutions: Cedars Sinai—where the psychiatrist had once seen me for 25 cents— and the Simon Wiesenthal Center's Museum of Tolerance, which was looking for survivors to tell their personal stories.

Speaking at the museum was a difficult step. I had never been comfortable speaking in public, even to just a few people. As I prepared for my first speech, I felt so nervous I had knots in my stomach. My doctor prescribed Valium to help me calm down. That helped, but the experience took an unexpected emotional toll. I felt so weak afterwards that I came home and got in bed. At the same time, I felt gratified. The next time, I skipped the Valium and took two Tylenol. And after that, I was on my own. I became stronger and better.

Since then, I have spoken almost every week at the museum—to school groups, tourists, church groups. I have told my story at interfaith religious services, churches, and universities. I speak to educators, to law-enforcement officers, and sometimes via videoconference to teenagers in juvenile detention facilities.

I have never turned down an invitation, and never accepted a penny for my work.

People sometimes ask me how I can torture myself by reliving the worst moments of my life over and over. They ask: How can you do that?

I can because it gives me a sense of purpose. For years, I lived in the past. I carried a heavy heart and so many painful memories, but I only rarely expressed what I was thinking.

Now, every time I tell my story, it is as if I am bringing back a piece of Putnok, and parts of Mother and Father and my six siblings. Every time a new audience hears of my experiences, I feel that not only have I survived, but so does a piece of the past.

God had a purpose for me. In sharing my story, I am living out a purposeful life.

Every audience is different, but I hear many of the same questions repeatedly. Some of the children's questions show innocence and a uniquely childlike perspective:

"Did you meet Hitler?"

"Did you meet Anne Frank?"

"Why didn't you become more crazy?"

Some of the children ask to see my tattoo or the scar from my dog bite. I always show them. It makes it that much more real for them.

One thing that always fascinates the children is hearing about my pet, Riley. Nancy and my granddaughter, Kimberly, brought him home from a shelter just after Ernie died in 1997. I was just returning home from a bar mitzvah when they surprised me with a dog, and not just any dog: a German shepherd.

"I'm terrified," I said. I immediately thought of the ferocious hounds in Auschwitz. But Nancy soothed my nerves.

"You'll make peace with her," she said, assuring me Riley was a gentle, loving dog.

Now people ask: "How could you have a German shepherd?"

Having the dog truly helped me to heal and move on, to realize that just as not all German shepherds are trained and vicious killers, we can't generalize about Germans, either. A dog is just a dog. A person is just a person.

Often, the questions are more challenging.

When people hear about my religious background, many of them—Jews, Christians, Moslems, atheists—have the same question: How could God have let this happen?

I conclude that God wasn't responsible. It's people who did the damage. God gave each of us the capacity to choose between good and evil. With less energy, you can do good. It takes more effort to do evil—whether you cheat or lie or fight. The Torah teaches that God created people in His image, to be perfect. We could be perfect, but none of us are. We all have faults. We have the ability to make choices. If you do good, you help the world. If you help yourself, God will help you.

We all have faults. Any teacher will tell you, there are one or two bullies in every classroom. If you don't stop them, those bullies will become vicious leaders. Nobody stopped Hitler.

The God I believe in is the God who was with me in the cattle car and in Auschwitz, the God who stayed with me in the airplane factory in Augsburg and on the death march. The God who brought me back to my father. Through it all, I felt God's presence. I said a lot of prayers.

"God," I would say, "I just know you are going to take care of me." That faith came from growing up in a religious home. And it gave me great strength.

Another question comes up almost every time I speak. If they have never met a survivor—or, more often, if they have—people tell me they expected someone full of anger, someone who is mostly looking to lay blame. But I don't express much anger. I try to give hope. Especially when people hear how I responded to the American soldier who asked me to point out the SS men for punishment, they always want do know: "Why did you let them go? Where is your anger?"

I don't forget what the Germans did, but I've tried to forgive them, and mostly I have tried to let it go, to move on.

"Forgive the Nazis?" survivors ask me. "How could you?"

Forgiveness doesn't mean I approve of what they did or that they're not guilty of crimes. But I don't want to carry that heavy heart, that burden—to be occupied constantly with hatred. If you focus so much on hatred, you cannot be a loving wife or a loving parent or a loving friend.

The best answer for me was just to turn the page and move on.

The SS men in Auschwitz and the ones who taunted me on the death march—they were following orders. Their leaders told them to go to the camps, beat the prisoners, train dogs to be mean and vicious. They did what they were told to do. Some of them enjoyed it more than others. They did horrible things but they were fighting for their country.

Should I carry on with the hatred? It's over. The Nazis can't do anything more to me. Nor can I turn back the clock so that it didn't happen. It *did* happen. We suffered. We lost so many, many people.

But I have always thought of what Father taught me: If you save one life, you have saved the whole world.

I never wanted to harm the Germans. I just wanted to move on and rebuild my life. And even looking back after 60 years, I'm glad that I just said, "I want to go home. I want to find my family. I want to fall in love, get married, have children—and never forget."

When you forgive, it is a gift to yourself. The person who committed the crime rarely cares whether you hate them or love them. But it was a gift to myself not to carry that burden.

When I was still very young I had to decide: Am I going to live with hatred, or am I going to find peace within my heart? I chose to be a peaceful person. And that has helped me.

Where did that come from? In part, it was from the teachings of my Father—the Torah stories he shared with us on Shabbat afternoons, the sermons I watched him deliver in our shul in Putnok. And the way he lived his life. I'm sure it came, too, from the Germans I met in the Augsburg factory—men and women doing what they had been told to do but still, in the midst of that nightmare, able to treat other people as human beings.

And partly it is just my nature. I don't like being angry or hearing loud voices. I try to avoid fights. I have always felt that if you talk things over in a diplomatic way, you accomplish more than if you call each other names or spit on each other or kick and hit. I just never wanted any part of that. For me, the best solution was to remember, to never forget, but to move on and rebuild my life. And that helped me become a more loving, caring, compassionate person.

Often, people in my audiences tell me what a noble thing I have done, likening me to Pope John Paul II, who forgave the man who shot him. I see it as much more basic. I do not see myself as extraordinary. I am not an iron woman. I have illnesses. I get upset; I become emotional. I have a lot of anxiety. I have nightmares. But I carry on, because I know that God selected me for a reason: to come home and rebuild my life and remember my family and the others who have no voice. I take that mission seriously.

I am here for a reason, and part of it is to carry on my parents' work in the world. I feel them almost every day. I know that if Father were here, he would recognize parts of himself in me. And I am proud of that. I know that having faith and religion makes you a more well-rounded, decent person.

Father always told me: "If you go by 'An eye for an eye,' the whole world will be blind."

Keeping that in mind has helped me to move on and make a difference in the world.

My mother's words, too, echo in my mind. So many things she told me to reassure me in dark times came true. Not long ago, I spoke at a Catholic college in Los Angeles. I was hesitant to tell the story of what happened the first day I had to go out wearing a yellow star as a child—how the two nuns spit on my mother and me. I didn't want to be insensitive. But I also wanted to tell the truth.

As I told it, I noticed two nuns in the audience, who began to cry.

Afterwards, they approached me.

"We feel terrible for what you went through," they said. "We're sorry for what happened." They both embraced me. They gave me a blessing and said they would pray for me.

I felt a chill. Mother had promised me that someday people would apologize for what they had done to us. And here I was accepting an apology.

I keenly felt her presence another time. When I still worked as a library technician, I was at the public desk when a middle-aged man came in to register for a library card. As he was filling out the application form, I noticed he was dripping with sweat. I glanced at his name on the application and noticed it was German. I realized he had seen the tattoo on my arm, and he was almost shaking. I quietly pushed a buzzer to alert a colleague to come and take over the desk. I didn't want to humiliate him.

I went to the back, but after he was finished, I returned to the desk. After he checked out his books with his new card, he approached me at the counter.

"Ma'am, I was very upset," he told me. "I happened to notice your tattoo number on your arm. I am from Germany. " He told me he was the German consul, stationed in Los Angeles for one year. "I have never stood so close to a survivor of the Holocaust. I am so ashamed of my ancestors and what they did to you."

I listened, taken aback.

"I want to apologize for what happened to you," he said.

And then he did something I will never forget: He grabbed my left arm and kissed the tattoo.

I stood there, locked, paralyzed. Again I thought about my mother and what she had said the morning the nuns spit on us: Someday, they will apologize. I felt so connected to her. That day at the library, she was right there beside me.

LOOKING BACK AT HOW MUCH we endured, it's a miracle that anyone came back. I never imagined the idyllic world of my childhood would ever come to an end. How could I? How could I visualize losing my mother? Or my siblings or grandparents? Or that I could lose so many of them and that life would go on? Even now, when I speak of losing 60 members of my family, I don't know how I was able to move on.

How could I laugh again? How could I lead a normal life, get married, raise children, hold a job and be a productive citizen without those 60 people? How could I survive without my country, my culture, my language? Everything?

Somehow I did and I became an old woman.

Here is what I always say in the face of loss—however small or overwhelming. It's not what you lost. It's what you still have. I lost so much—but not everything. They could never take my soul away. They didn't take my memory. No matter what they do to you, if you have your soul, you're still a human being. You can rebuild your life.

Let me repeat that:

It's not what you lost. It's what you still have.

My treasured possessions are gone: Father's war diary and his *siddur*—and nearly every beloved soul whose name he had written inside its cover.

But I have this story.

I STILL VISIT FATHER'S GRAVE twice a year: on his *yartzheit*—the Hebrew anniversary of his death—and in the autumn, around the time of the Jewish High Holidays.

That plot is my link to the past—to the house in Putnok lined with shelves of Hebrew texts, to the lively Shabbat dinners filled with song and so much food, to my mother and siblings who have no graves. It is the one piece of land where I can go and remember all of that.

That is also where I think of how I want to be remembered. There's a plot right next to Father's for me. I have told my daughters what they should get carved on my tombstone. First, my three Jewish names, and my English name. Father always told me I was an *Eyshes Chayil*—the words from Proverbs for a woman of valor. So I'll have that, too.

I want it to say: "Eva Rosenfeld Brown. *Bracha Hinde Leah. Eyshes Chayil.* Holocaust Survivor. Daughter, Wife, Mother, Grandmother."

And one more thing.

I want the stone to have my tattoo number: A17923. They tried to turn me into a number, but I won't just go away quietly and die.

I want the world to know a Holocaust survivor lived on to be as old as God lets me live.

I came back and rebuilt my life.

And I will be part of history forever.

Responses

THOUSANDS OF THE CHILDREN AND ADULTS who have heard me speak have taken the time to send me cards and letters—many of them personal and moving. It is gratifying to hear of the impact of my story, as expressed here in a few excerpts.

> "Your story had me crying all the way home from class. I came from Vietnam and lost part of my family during the Vietnam war in 1975. Because I had lost part of my family, I find it hard to forgive the North Vietnamese. But after listening to how you made peace with your enemies and forgive them even when they had killed half of your family, I came to realize the hate that I hold inside of me. ... Your words are like gold to me."
> —*Tammy, college student*

> "One thing that I am never going to forget is how you did not want to point at those that had maltreated you when the American soldiers asked you. You explained that 'hatred is self-destruction'

and that your father always said, 'If you save one life, you save the world.' You, Mrs. Brown, have saved many worlds with your story and warm heart. "

— *Maria, college student*

"I went straight home and shared your memories with my own child. I could never imagine my child having to be as brave as you were at such a young age. . . . I had so many questions I wanted to ask you. How does one have such forgiveness for those that have created such pain? I wish I knew."

— *Beverly, college student*

"After the nuns treated you and your mother so rudely that day, it is inspiring that you look beyond their faults and have come to speak at a Catholic institution."

— *Jessica, college student*

"You mentioned that you do not hold any hate in your heart over the things that were done to you and your family. How can this be? This is something that I struggle with in my own life. It has left me in awe of your capacity to see the good in this world."

— *Jennifer, college student*

"My favorite part of your story was when you said that you and your best friend promised to stick together and help each other out. It would make me feel much safer to know that I had someone there with me."

— *Lauren, high-school student*

"Your story has made me realize that I can't always hate people for their actions or bad ways, but sometimes it's hard to move on with your life when you think of how people tend to treat you. I do understand that I must learn to move on without holding any grudges on my back or shoulders. The only thing I don't understand is how you can forgive someone that has ruined your family and life so hatefully."

—*Robin, high-school student*

"I had a situation that involved hate not too long ago. It involved fighting. Now I realize that I didn't learn anything by the way I acted. The only thing that I got was pride for about five minutes. After my anger cooled down I was just left with a couple of bruises and my pride was gone. Now I notice that fighting was not the answer and I have to learn to forgive. I will always remember the message you gave us: 'You must forgive, you cannot be a full person if you have hatred in your heart.'"

—*Jonathan, high-school student*

"There is only one person that has made me feel miserable during my 17 years I have been alive but in my case I never knew the person, but I think in order for that person to stay out of my mind is to forgive him. Ms. Eva that person that I have to forgive is my father; can you please give me some advice on whether I should forgive him or not. I would really appreciate it."

—*Alvaro, high-school student*

"The thing that affected me the most about your story is that they did not give you guys nothing to drink and expected you to walk such a long walk while you licked each other to keep cool....I will always remember not to be the way they were and will never let hate take me over."
—*Brittany, high-school student*

"When I was in second grade, a fourth grader bullied me because I was different. He continued harassing me until he graduated from the school. I hated that guy til this day, because of what he has done to me. Then when you told everyone, 'It's better to forgive, but don't forget,' I felt like some part of me, the hatred part, was lifting away, and I knew you were right. I will always remember that quote and the person that got it through my head."
—*Sarath, high-school student*

"Thanks to you I realize that 'hating' an individual is destructive behavior, and I will do my best to 'dislike' those I disagree with."
—*Jafarzadeh, high-school student*

"Many times I have asked myself, 'Why me?' especially when I have problems that are too hard for me to face. I listened to you recount those gruesome, horrible details...and I feel great admiration for you. You had such great courage, valor, and faith in yourself, which kept you alive. Like you said, the human spirit is great and it is something that cannot be destroyed."
—*Sonia, college student*

"Your story of the tomato and your mother reminded me of how much I love my parents and how they will not always be around. The first thing I did when I got out of class was to call my parents, my sister and my boyfriend just to let them know I was thinking of them. Thank you for reminding me of those important lessons."

—*Blair, college student*

"The part that touched me was when you said that you reunited with your father. After you said that I saw your face light up with happiness and joy like when a little kid opens up his Christmas present."

—*Richard, high-school student*

"I was surprised…that you forgave the people that had done this to you, that you had no hate for what was done to your people. My people, the Armenians, have experienced genocide of their own. Of course I was not a part of it, but I feel as though I was there, and I feel the pain that my people went through. I don't think that I could ever forgive the people that are responsible…."

—*Hakop, high-school student*

"I learned that if you have faith, you can get through the toughest times."

—*Lillian, fourth grader*

With El Camino College
President Thomas Fallo.

An Address to Students

Of the hundreds of speeches I've given, one of the highlights was delivering the commencement speech at El Camino College in Torrance, California on June 9, 2006.

WHEN I WAS ASKED TO BE a keynote speaker at your graduation, I was immediately overcome by amazement and dread. Amazement that I, a foreigner with a sixth-grade education, was chosen to inspire you. And dread that I would not be able to.

I have spent a lot of time worrying over what I could possibly say to you that would mark this momentous occasion. What would you take from this? Our differences are so great—you are at least sixty years my junior and have at least fourteen years of education. You have mastered the electronic world of computers, digital cameras, and cell phones. I can hunt and peck on a typewriter, take photos with my Kodak and would never give up my rotary

147

phone. But the biggest difference is our education: You are graduating from college and I graduated from Auschwitz. Still, if your enemies are your teachers, I have learned so much from the Nazis.

To understand my message, you must know my story. Seventy-nine years ago, I was the middle child born to a rabbi and his wife in a very small town in Hungary. My childhood was spent with my eight brothers and sisters. Life was simple and carefree. We played, went to school and celebrated holidays, But in the midst of this normalcy, German boots were marching across Europe. In 1944 Hungary was invaded and my life was turned upside down as my father was taken away to a labor camp. My mother, younger siblings and I were sent to the ghetto. Struggling with hunger and exhaustion, I did not think things could get worse until the cattle cars came and took us to Auschwitz, a place of unimaginable horrors and atrocities—and ferocious beauty and tenacity of the human spirit. It is a bizarre coincidence that this occurred on June 9th, exactly sixty-two years ago, on a Friday night.

As I watched my mother and siblings led to the gas chamber, I could not understand the depravity and madness of human beings reflected in Hitler's "Final Solution." Everyone's past was erased. No distinction was made between doctors, lawyers, teachers, shoemakers and honors students: Each identity was reduced to a blue tattoo number branded on our forearms.

I found solace in the compassion of the Nazi guard who brought me food and a blanket to shield me from the bitter cold. I learned that to make myself valuable was to live. At 15 years of age, I had expected to be dating, going to school and planning a dazzling future. Instead I concentrated on discovering talents that would keep me alive: giving manicures, haircuts and massages to my captors. I became an experimental scientist of my own body and mind. I learned to stay awake during the daily 4 a.m. head count that lasted three hours. I carefully balanced my food intake and energy output so I was able to finish all my work. Death was certain for those who fell asleep or behind in their assignments.

Even under these dehumanizing conditions, we had choices. Some committed suicide by throwing themselves on the electric barbed-wire; others overcame starvation and sickness by sheer force of will in their determination to live. We prayed and comforted each other and vowed to make sure that one day the world would know what happened to us.

I learned psychology—especially the art of denial and distance. I dreamt of my future. Looking beyond the smoke from the gas chambers, I planned my life. I would find my family, get married, buy a house and have children. I selected my wardrobe and menus—visions of shiny silk dresses, warm woolen coats, stuffed goose and rich pastries filled my head as I removed gold teeth from dead prisoners. I named my smiling, healthy children as I clipped the German officers' mustaches and I danced with my dashing husband as I filed their nails. I designed my living room and chose wall paper for my bedroom as I worked outside in my bare feet as icy rain and snow soaked through me.

After liberation, I reunited with my father and learned that sixty members of my family had perished during the war. At seventeen, I was struggling to regain footing in a world that had been pulled from under my feet. I read a book written by a Hungarian author about Auschwitz. Seized by an overwhelming desire to tell my version, I immediately began to organize my thoughts on just how my story would unfold. I told my father that I wanted to capture my experience in my own book. He somberly looked at me and intoned, "Life will never be the same. It will just be an imitation of life. You need to rebuild your life and not live in the past. Don't ever talk about it." A dutiful daughter, my inspiration turned to surrender.

I followed my father's wishes and left for America with nothing but a desire to rebuild. I had lost my family, my country, an entire lifestyle. But I married, raised two children and learned to speak a new language. I worked, paid taxes and gave to charity. My fellow survivors and family never talked about our experiences. It was like a bad dream we forgot after waking up in America.

In the media, the Holocaust was sensationalized or sentimentalized—it did not ring true. I remembered the fear in the young Nazi guard's eyes as he reluctantly carried out his orders. I recalled how the Catholic nuns turned their backs as we begged for their help in the ghetto. I was haunted by the memory of the six million who did not survive. Only a witness to behavior in extremity could convey the wrenching reality. In 1994 I saw *Schindler's List* and was transported back to that terrible time and place. As I watched the survivors pay tribute to the man who saved them, I vowed to break my silence. After waiting fifty years, I was finally ready to tell my story. While I could not speak for the dead, I would honor their memory by sharing my experiences. And so I became a teller of stories.

I volunteered to give testimoy for the Shoah Foundation and the Museum of Tolerance. Speaking as a Jew who comes from far away, I share my family's story with a diverse audience: Catholics, Muslims and agnostics, young and old. I speak of loss and redemption, of the evil that people are capable of and the good with which they can heal. The Nazis taught me the power of forgiveness. This enables me to spread my message of tolerance and respect for everyone. People from all walks of life relate to my experiences. I have found that faith and age are not the common denominators. It is by being part of the human family with the realms of emotions that tough us all— grief, terror, despair, joy—that people embrace my determination to ensure that the world will never forget what happened over sixty years ago.

My story is also about the randomness of how we're placed in life and how we respond. The greatest lesson that I have learned is captured in a quote by Albert Einstein: "There are only two ways to live your life. One is as though nothing is a miracle. The other is as though everything is a miracle." The fact that I am celebrating here today with you confirms that I am living the latter.

Sixty years ago, the world ignored the genocide of the Jews. Today, in America, 25 states require the Holocaust to be taught and 24 others implicitly encourage it. My life has come full circle. I enjoyed so many opportunities here and always felt that I was riding on a train without a ticket. There was a larger debt to be repaid. For a family that journeyed to this country for freedom, I am finally paying the fare.

And so my message to you is to never give up. Follow your dreams and always have hope. Be involved in your life through your family, friends and public service. Play a role in making your community and your country safe, so that every citizen may enjoy their freedom just as I have.

WHEREAS, Eva Brown, is a champion of human rights and social justice; and

WHEREAS, Eva Brown stands as a symbol of hope, possibilities, and promises for a life which is dedicated to social change; and

WHEREAS, Eva Brown has not chosen a life of leisure but rather one of dedication in spreading the message of hope and tolerance and forgiveness and justice for all; and

NOW, THEREFORE, BE IT RESOLVED, that El Camino College does hereby award this Proclamation to Eva Brown on this day, Friday, June 9, 2006.

Presented during the Fifty-Ninth Annual Commencement Ceremony at El Camino College the ninth day of June in the year Two Thousand and Six.

Thomas M. Fallo
Superintendent/President

El Camino College honored me with this proclamation.